CALLED AND ACCOUNTABLE

Other books in the "Called and Accountable" series

Called and Accountable:
Discovering Your Place in God's Eternal Purpose
(Bible study, revised edition)
Henry T. Blackaby and Norman C. Blackaby

El llamado de Dios:
El propósito de Dios para todo creyente
(Called and Accountable: God's Purpose for Every Believer)
Henry T. Blackaby and Kerry L. Skinner
Translated by Miguel Mesías

CALLED AND ACCOUNTABLE

Discovering Your Place
in God's Eternal Purpose

Henry T. Blackaby
and
Norman C. Blackaby

NEW HOPE
PUBLISHERS

Birmingham, Alabama

New Hope® Publishers
P. O. Box 12065
Birmingham, AL 35202-2065
www.newhopepublishers.com

Library of Congress Cataloging-in-Publication Data

Blackaby, Henry T., 1935-
Called and accountable : discovering your place in God's eternal
purpose / Henry T. Blackaby and Norman C. Blackaby.
    p. cm.
Includes bibliographical references and index.
ISBN 978-1-59669-047-9 (jacketed hard cover : alk. paper)
  1. Vocation Christianity. I. Blackaby, Norman C. II. Title.
BV4740.B57 2007
248.4—dc22
        2006035170

ISBN-10: 1-59669-047-X
ISBN-13: 978-1-59669-047-9

N064153 • 0407 • 12M1

DEDICATION

To my uncle and his wife, Lorimer and Olive Baker,
who faithfully served as missionaries in Manchuria, China,
working with Jonathan Goforth
during the great Shantung Revival,
and who baptized me as a nine-year-old boy and later
became my pastor when God called me into the ministry.
—HENRY BLACKABY

To my wife, Dana, with gratitude to our Lord,
for your love and support.
—NORMAN BLACKABY

TABLE OF CONTENTS

PREFACE

The message found in the pages of *Called and Accountable* has been on our hearts for many years. In 1986, I [Henry] was asked to speak at a retreat in Toccoa, Georgia. This conference was of particular significance in that it shaped the direction of the rest of my ministry and the life of my family. At this retreat, I preached four sermons: "All Are Called," "All Are Gifted," "All Are Sent," and, in conclusion, "How to Hear God." I was asked to put the teachings from the last session into writing; this eventually became the workbook *Experiencing God*. The teachings of the first three sessions were put into a small 35-page book titled *Called and Accountable*; this was turned into a workbook that has been enlarged and completely revised recently (2005).

The overwhelmingly positive response to the newly rewritten *Called and Accountable* workbook has been the impetus for this book. As Norman has preached and taught this message across North America and as Called and Accountable Weekends have been established, we sensed a need for a "read-through" book separate from the workbook. This book follows the chapter titles of the workbook and includes the significant subtitles, but it does not attempt to follow the daily readings and topics of the workbook. It is our hope and prayer that this book will be an encouragement to many of God's people to wholeheartedly live out God's call upon their lives, and we pray that studying *Called and Accountable* will result in each reader being enabled to *"walk worthy of the calling with which [they] were called"* (Ephesians 4:1).

—HENRY BLACKABY AND NORMAN BLACKABY

January 2007

INTRODUCTION

As we travel and minister around the world, we see so many of God's precious people who deeply want their lives to be used by God in a significant way in His kingdom. Often, they hear stories of how God is using other people on the missions field or in the city in which they live, and they wonder if God could somehow use their lives to make a difference. Others we talk with struggle to express what they are feeling, but share that they sense there must be more to the Christian life than they are experiencing. They do not know what it is they are missing, but they have a yearning for more.

We continue to meet many people who relate that God has been opening up their eyes to the fact that there is more to life than working 40 to 60 hours a week and taking their families to church on Sundays. It is as if God has been calling them out saying, "The world has had My children long enough to help it be more successful, while My kingdom goes wanting. I am calling My people back to Myself to use them for My purposes and My kingdom." Some are being called right out of the marketplace to serve in full-time ministry positions. However, more often, God is not removing His people from the workplace, but reorienting them to Himself so that they begin to see their workplaces from

God's perspective. For the first time for many of His children, the workplace is not simply a career or occupation for them, but a place where God has called them to walk with eyes fixed on Him and His work.

In our day, a growing distinction has developed between believers in Christ who serve God in a "full-time Christian position," such as a pastor, missionary, or church staff person, and those who are typical members of a church who work out in the world during the week. Often persons in the first group are referred to respectfully as *called* into ministry, whereas those in the latter group are in some ways considered to be in a lesser position. No doubt, the Bible distinguishes different types of roles in the church; however, the Scriptures designate every believer in Christ as *called* by God. In a letter to the Christians at the church in Rome, the Apostle Paul wrote, *"You also are the called of Jesus Christ"* (Romans 1:6). Paul continually charged believers to *"walk worthy of the calling"* they had received from God (Ephesians 4:1), and he prayed that God would count them *"worthy of this calling"* (2 Thessalonians 1:11). And it was not just a few in the church who were called, but *every believer* in Christ was called by God and, therefore, responsible to *"walk worthy of the calling."*

It is overwhelming to realize that the God of the universe, the only God and Creator of all that is, has chosen to call every believer into a very special relationship with Himself. This call and the relationship that follows are very personal and very real! The truth of this is found throughout the entire Bible—in life after life and verse after verse. It is central to the entire message of the Bible. It is, in fact, an expression of the very heart of God.

Even more amazing is the knowledge that it was God's choice to call people into such a personal relationship with Himself: *"He chose us in Him [Christ] before the foundation of the world, that we should be holy and without blame before Him in love"* (Ephesians 1:4). Jesus expressed the will of the Father to His disciples this way: *"You did not choose Me, but I chose you and appointed you that you should go and bear fruit, and that your fruit should remain, that whatever you ask the Father in My name He may give you"* (John 15:16). This truth remains to this day and includes each of us.

When this reality grips a person's heart, he or she is never the same again. Immediately there comes into that life a deep sense of meaning and purpose and a sense of stewardship, or accountability, to God. So personal and real was this to King David that he said to God:

> *My frame was not hidden from You,*
> *When I was made in secret,*
> *And skillfully wrought in the lowest parts of the earth.*
> *Your eyes saw my substance, being yet unformed.*
> *And in Your book they all were written,*
> *The days fashioned for me,*
> *When as yet there were none of them.*

How precious also are Your thoughts to me, O God!
How great is the sum of them!
—Psalm 139:15–17

Jeremiah also was made aware of this calling, purpose, and accountability, because the Lord God informed him:

"Before I formed you in the womb I knew you;
Before you were born I sanctified you;
I ordained you a prophet to the nations."
—Jeremiah 1:5

God then unfolded to Jeremiah what this would mean to him, and the stewardship of this knowledge radically affected the rest of his life.

To provide another picture of this truth, we can look at the witness of the Apostle Paul as he related what God had revealed to him: "God . . . *separated me from my mother's womb and called me through His grace*" (Galatians 1:15). Much of the Book of Acts is the record of what this call of God meant for Paul's life. Such love of God, Paul said, literally "constrained" him (*constrained him* means ordered all of the rest of his life). In this special relationship with God, Paul increasingly became convinced that "*He [Christ Jesus] died for all, that those who live should live no longer for themselves, but for Him who died for them and rose again*" (2 Corinthians 5:15). Paul expressed what this meant in his life by saying, *"But by the grace of God I am what I am, and His grace toward me was not in vain; but I labored more abundantly than they all, yet not I, but the grace of God which was with me"* (1 Corinthians 15:10), thus expressing his enormous sense of accountability to God for such love toward him.

Again, this sense of call and accountability was not limited in the New Testament to just a few special people. Every believer is spoken of as the called of God, or the chosen of God, or ones set apart by God! As the Scriptures are our guide for both faith and practice (or daily living), this truth and its implication for each of our lives will guide us thoroughly in our relationship with God. Therefore, as we seek God's wisdom throughout this book, our prayer is that the Holy Spirit will help us understand and respond to God. In this pursuit, we will look at six questions:

1. **WHY** DOES GOD CALL US?
2. **WHAT** IS A CALL?
3. **WHO** ARE THE CALLED?
4. **HOW** AM I CALLED?
5. **WHEN** AM I CALLED?
6. **HOW** DO I LIVE OUT THE CALL?

Because this book was written with the intent to encourage God's people to live out the call God has placed upon their lives, we have included many examples of Christians who have lived faithfully toward the Lord in the past and many who are currently serving alongside of Christ. It is our hope that these examples will serve as a challenge and reminder that God continues to choose ordinary people to be involved with Him in extraordinary work.

As you read this book, you will notice that we instruct you to record the truths you are learning in a spiritual journal. Keeping a journal of God's activity and His words to you is vital for your continued growth and understanding of God activity. So grab a notebook or journal, and let's get started!

CHAPTER 1

Why Does God Call Us?

ESSENTIAL TRUTH

No one can adequately come to knowledge of God's truth, for themselves or for others, without a thorough commitment to the place and authority of God's Word (the Bible). It is in the Scriptures that God has chosen to reveal Himself and His will for our lives. As a person approaches the Bible and opens its pages, he or she comes face-to-face with the author—God! The Holy Spirit is present to open the mind and heart of the child of God to an immediate word from God for that person's life (John 14:16–17; John 16:13–15; 1 Corinthians 2:10–16). Without this commitment to encounter God in His Word, one is left to human reasoning alone—something that will never lead to God or an understanding of His Word. This entire study is based on the assumption that the reader is committed to meet God in His Word and respond to Him in this encounter.

> *And whatever you do, do it heartily, as to the Lord and not to men, knowing that from the Lord you will receive the reward of the inheritance; for you serve the Lord Christ.*
> —COLOSSIANS 3:23–24

G. R. S. Blackaby

Testimony from Henry Blackaby About His Father

I knew my dad as a very ordinary businessman who was a committed Christian in his workplace. He was born in England and immigrated to Canada as a young man, seeking adventure in Canada. He began to work for the Bank of Montreal and soon became a branch manager. He was moved regularly, but he always sought to be an open Christian wherever he was placed.

Early in his life, he knew that God had a special place for him—where and what it was, he did not know at the time. But the fact that he would be faithful to his Lord was obvious. As I was growing up, I watched him witness to all who came into his life: to the down and out, to the businessmen with whom he worked, and to anyone he came into contact with in the city where he lived. He was, to me, the greatest soul winner I have ever known. Because of his faithful witness and conscientious walk with God, he was recognized as a Christian with integrity in every city or town where he lived.

Dad was always bringing people into our home. As he would enter, he would ask us to pray for him and his guest because he was going to share with this person about the Lord. He would then appear in the doorway a little while later and say that his guest had something he wanted to say. We had come to know that, through the tears, this person would tell us he had received Christ into his life, and we would rejoice together.

My father, who was a deacon, knew that every deacon should preach, teach, lead others in prayer, and begin a church if there was not one available. He started a church in a dance hall and preached every Sunday until (after several years) we finally got a pastor. He was an ordinary man, a businessman, who let God use him in countless ways to make Christ known. After his death, my brothers and I had many people come up to us and tell us that our dad was the finest Christian they ever knew. They would add some personal experience like "He made a loan to me—on character and with prayer" or "He was the only one who believed in me, and I am what I am today because of your godly father." What a heritage we have because of my dad's faithfulness.

Our home was a place of prayer for all peoples. This was especially true of the native First Nations believers from the surrounding reserves. On our knees, we prayed for a mighty move of God among these dear people. My own sense of call into the ministry and my life commitment to the native peoples came from my godly father's influence.

I saw that an ordinary child of God could be greatly used of God—unnoticed by much of the world, but known in heaven. Many children, youth, and adults will be in heaven for eternity because of the faithful witness of my father, an ordinary businessman.

God Works Through His People

The entire Bible bears witness to the truth that God, from eternity, chose to work through His people to accomplish His eternal purposes in the world. He could have worked out everything by Himself, just as He worked during the Creation, but He chose not to do it that way. Rather, the Bible tells how God called individuals into a special relationship with Himself so that He could use them to accomplish His purposes.

When God was about to destroy every living thing from the earth because of sin, He called Noah to Himself and, through Noah, preserved his family and enough living creatures to begin to populate the earth again (Genesis 6–10). When God wanted to establish saving faith (salvation) for all mankind, He chose Abram, whose name He changed to Abraham, to be the one He would shape to be a sample of that faith to the end of time (Genesis 12–22; Hebrews 11:8). When God was ready to deliver His chosen people from bondage in Egypt, He called Moses to Himself and sent him to be the one through whom He would accomplish this task (Exodus 3). The New Testament is filled with examples of God choosing people to be used to accomplish His purposes. The choosing of the Twelve and the call of the Apostle Paul are the most obvious examples.

A quick look at our church history reveals numerous examples of God calling out and using people to bring about His purposes. When, in God's timing, He desired the Bible to be translated into the common language of the English-speaking world, He raised up William Tyndale for the task. There was a time when God's people had moved away from the understanding and role of grace in the Christian life. At that time, God chose to radically impact the life of Martin Luther to call the people back to a salvation by grace, through faith.

The people God called were carpenters, fishermen, farmers, shepherds, servants, and businesspeople.

When God's people had lost sight of the truth that God was a God who heard and answered prayer, He called out George Müller to a ministry to orphans that would impact the world through the example of faithfulness to prayer and God's answer and provision.

We can read the examples in Scripture and often not make the connection to our own lives. It is easy to look at the people used in Scripture and see them as larger than life. We can forget that at the time when God called these people, they were ordinary people who simply had a heart that was obedient to God when He called. The people God called were carpenters, fishermen, farmers, shepherds, servants, and businesspeople. Looking at them after God accomplished His work through their lives, we do not see them this way, but they would have seen themselves as very ordinary in their day.

Through the years, God has chosen to use ordinary people to accomplish His purposes, and He continues to do so in our day. Does He need us to accomplish His work? Certainly not! However, God has determined to involve His people. He calls individuals He can trust to be the instruments through which He will accomplish His eternal purposes. In John 15:16, Jesus put it this way: *"You did not choose Me, but I chose you and appointed you that you should go and bear fruit, and that your fruit should remain."* When God chose you (Ephesians 1:4), He did so with the purpose that your life would bear fruit or, we could say, with the purpose of using your life to accomplish His purposes.

At times, God looks for someone to use, but does not find anyone who is willing or who is living in a way that God could trust them with His work. When God does not have someone who will allow his or her life to be used, serious consequences often follow. One well-known example of this is found in Ezekiel:

> *"So I sought for a man among them who would make a wall, and stand in the gap before Me on behalf of the land, that I should not destroy it; but I found no one. Therefore I have poured out My indignation on them; I have consumed them with the fire of My wrath; and I have recompensed their deeds on their own heads,"* says the Lord GOD.
>
> —EZEKIEL 22:30–31

This is a most solemn truth revealed by God so that each of us will take seriously any invitation of God to be His instrument. It may be to share God's love with our families or neighbors or to take part in missions projects. The eternal destiny of others may rest in our responses to His call, and the Bible makes it clear that He will hold us accountable for our responses.

God does not want His people to suffer judgment; rather, He wants His people to honor Him and receive His blessing. In Ezekiel's day, God appointed him to warn the people of the pending danger of rebelling against God. In this assignment, God called Ezekiel *"a watchman"* for God's people. God also described the awesome responsibility of a watchman (Ezekiel 33:1–20). The watchman was responsible to watch a portion of the horizon from his station upon the wall. If an enemy was sighted, he was to blow the trumpet and warn the people of the danger. The watchman was not responsible for fighting the enemy or equipping the people, but to warn them. As the Book of Ezekiel unfolds this illustration, a spiritual application is seen. The prophet was to warn of the danger that was approaching because of the people's sin. Once Ezekiel had God's message for His people, he was accountable for delivering that word. The prophet was not accountable for the way the people responded to the warning, but only for being a faithful messenger.

> *"Then whoever hears the sound of the trumpet and does not take warning, if the sword comes and takes him away, his blood shall be on his own head. . . . But if the watchman sees the sword coming and does not blow the trumpet, and the people are not warned, and the sword comes and takes any*

person from among them, he is taken away in his iniquity;
but his blood I will require at the watchman's hand."

—EZEKIEL 33:4, 6

This same truth applies to every Christian today. God has placed His people as watchmen and watchwomen in the home, the workplace, the church, and neighborhoods. They are to share the good news of God's Word as well as to share the danger of rejecting God's invitation to salvation. Every Christian must recognize the serious accountability presented in Ezekiel 33:1–20 and apply it to their own lives today. This is why it is imperative that we believe the Scriptures. They reveal God and His ways, so that when God approaches us, we will know that it is God, know how to respond to God, and know the serious nature of the consequences of not responding.

It can be hard to make the connection between what Ezekiel was doing among the children of Israel and our own lives, but the cost of sin remains the same in our day as in the days of the Old Testament. God continues to place His people among the nations to speak a word of life and of warning.

FROM NORMAN: ENCOURAGING TEENS

Recently I was with a church teaching them about being called and accountable. As we began to open the Scriptures, several people shared a burden about teenagers in and around the church. During these days, so many teenagers make decisions that determine the entire course of their lives. As this group began to share, they made the comment that they did not know how to reach these kids. They felt they were simply ordinary people without seminary training. But the burden to help these youth was unmistakable. As we began to talk, one man shared his passion for classic cars, and another shared about his bass boat and love of fishing. It soon became obvious that God had put on their hearts to share with the youth, but the avenue to do it was not in the youth room of the church, but out fishing, driving in a classic car, and playing sports. God wanted them to share words of life, but when they did, the sharing did not look like that of an Old Testament prophet. It took the form of a middle-aged layperson sharing a hobby with a youth and talking about the goodness of God in the process. God can call you and use you in numerous ways to help and intercede for those around you. He simply needs your availability.

> *God can call you and use you in numerous ways to help and intercede for those around you. He simply needs your availability.*

FROM HENRY: BEING READY TO PRAY

Let me share an example of this truth from the life of my wife, Marilynn. When our children were teenagers, three of them were going to a youth event in Calgary, Alberta. At that time, we lived in Saskatoon, Saskatchewan. The boys would be driving about 300 miles with several others from our youth group. During the nighttime, as the boys were driving, God put a "warning" in Marilynn's heart concerning the safety of our boys. She sensed a deep urgency to pray for their safety while they were driving. She came to me and said, "Henry, we need to pray for the boys right now!" We stopped everything we were doing and prayed until God gave us peace that they were OK. When they arrived home, we asked them about their trip. They told us that a car coming from the other direction hit black ice on the highway and spun across the median into their lane. They continued, "But it was like God moved us out of the way!" We asked them at what time this had happened. It was the exact time that God had alerted Marilynn to pray for them. Marilynn was a watchperson for our family that night. Now, did Marilynn need to have formal training to be a watchman for our boys that night? No, she simply needed to have a heart open to the voice of God and a willingness to obey when He spoke.

> *So often we miss out on God's purposes for our lives because we are not alert or aware of the simple ways God intends to involve us in His work.*

So often we miss out on God's purposes for our lives because we are not alert or aware of the simple ways God intends to involve us in His work. Maybe, as you are reading these pages, you are becoming aware that you have not been a faithful watchperson where God has placed you. You have been looking for the spectacular assignments or have felt you needed more education when, in fact, God simply wanted your availability in prayer or for you to use a longtime hobby for His purposes. Stop and spend time asking God to forgive you, and release your life to be used by Him for His purposes today. Maybe God has asked you to be a watchperson, and you responded, "I don't feel qualified to do that." Remember that He needs only your heart and willingness, not your talents and abilities. The assignment could be as simple as waking up in the night to pray for someone or inviting your co-worker to a baseball game where a friendship can be created that enables you to share how exciting it is to know God personally. The ways in which God will use us is up to Him.

> *God needs only your heart and willingness, not your talents and abilities.*

When God comes to us, we need to have an open heart and an obedient life. One of the most significant illustrations of hearing and responding to God is found in the life of Mary, Jesus's mother. God's eternal purpose was to bring a Savior into the world and, through that Savior, to bring His great salvation to every person. He found the one through whom He would choose to work—Mary, a quiet young girl. An angel from God announced to her God's plan to use her for His purpose. Then came her amazing and wonderful response: *"'Behold the maid-servant of the Lord! Let it be to me according to your word.' And the angel departed from her"* (Luke 1:38). And God did what He said He would do! It was impossible for man, but possible with God (Luke 1:37). Mary had a heart that was perfect toward God, and God showed Himself strong on her behalf. *"For the eyes of the LORD run to and fro throughout the whole earth, to shew himself strong in the behalf of them whose heart is perfect toward him"* (2 Chronicles 16:9 KJV). This has been God's strategy from eternity—and still is with each of us today.

> *"For with God nothing will be impossible." Then Mary said, "Behold the maid-servant of the Lord! Let it be to me according to your word."*
>
> —LUKE 1:37–38

There are times when we are not given any details of God's plans for our lives except that He calls us to follow Him. In these situations, our hearts have to look like that of Levi (Matthew) in Luke 5. Jesus simply walked by Levi's tax booth and asked him to follow. No details were given, but we can assume that Levi knew who Jesus was and had heard all of the rumors of the teachings, preaching, and healings from the Lord. Levi knew enough that when the Lord called, he responded immediately: *"He left all, rose up, and followed Him"* (Luke 5:28).

God chooses to work through His people to accomplish His eternal purpose. He desires to use each of His children as watchpersons in their families, workplaces, communities, and throughout the world.

Prayer & Application

Have you arranged your life so that when God comes to you, you are ready and available to Him? If you would have to respond, "No, my life is not really in order to be used," then take time now to ask God to show you what changes you need to make to be available for His service.

Called: Not for Time, but for Eternity

In understanding the call of God in our lives, it is important to look at our lives and the world around us from God's perspective rather than through our own limited understanding. When God created us, He did not make us for time, but for eternity. As we get caught up in the events of the day or the scheduling of our time, it can be easy to forget this important truth. We were created in His image; this includes immortality (living for eternity).

Then God said, "Let Us make man in Our image, according to Our likeness. . . ."

So God created man in His own image; in the image of God He created him; male and female He created them.

—GENESIS 1:26–27

Jesus Himself declared constantly that the ones who believe in Him would have eternal life:

"Whoever believes in Him should not perish but have eternal life."

—JOHN 3:15

"My sheep hear My voice, and I know them, and they follow Me. And I give them eternal life, and they shall never perish; neither shall anyone snatch them out of My hand."

—JOHN 10:27–28

Paul also confirmed this truth by saying that when God saved us, He *"raised us up together, and made us sit together in the heavenly places in Christ Jesus"* (Ephesians 2:6), and that we were *"heirs of God and joint heirs with Christ"* (Romans 8:17). Thus, God's goal, His focus, is not time, but eternity. This life on earth is to prepare us for eternity. This was God's purpose from before the foundation of the world. This knowledge provides an understanding of why Jesus said to His disciples, *"Do not lay up for yourselves treasures on earth, . . . but lay up for yourselves treasures in heaven"* (Matthew 6:19–20).

As Christians, we know that when our earthly bodies die, we will spend eternity in heaven, but often we do not live as though we believe this truth. The Scriptures compare our lives on this earth to a vapor or to the flowers and grass, which are here today and gone tomorrow. When comparing our lives on this earth with our lives in heaven, the first is only a brief moment compared with an eternity in heaven. Because of this truth, upon what should we be placing our focus and energy? How much energy and time are we spending preparing for life in heaven? As we have asked Christians this question over the years, very few can share how they are investing in heavenly treasures. When we press it a bit further and make the comparison between the time spent preparing for our retirement on earth as opposed to the one in heaven, it becomes apparent that many Christians have not thought through the fact that they were created for eternity. We know that fact in our heads, but our actions often reveal that the truth has never settled in our hearts. Certainly it is important to invest and plan for our retirement upon this earth. With so many people living into their 90s these days, financial planning is needed for the later years of life. Yet what is a 20- to 30-year retirement compared with eternity? A vapor!

When God looks at our lives and the lives of those around us, He has eternity in mind. We need to have the same perspective.

He looks at the eternal destiny of each person and desires for each one to come into a deep, abiding fellowship with Him. Because God desires for every person to come to faith in Him through Christ Jesus, how should we view our relationships with people who do not know Christ? Many times we can relate to our co-workers and neighbors who are not Christians without any serious burden to share the gospel with them. We may pray for these people and even wish they would come to faith in Christ, but how seriously do we take into account their eternal destiny? God is burdened and actively at work in their lives, and as we gain His perspective, He will place this same burden upon us. To lay up treasures in heaven, we must walk worthy of our calling by investing in things that are eternal.

When God calls you to join Him, He is inviting you to be on mission with Him with eternity in mind. Evaluate your own life to see what you are investing in. Many Christians will pass from this life leaving all kinds of riches and accomplishments behind, only to find out that they spent the one life they had on the wrong things. The time that we have should be spent with "eternal investments" in the forefront of our hearts and minds. This is why Paul stated:

> And whatever you do, do it heartily, as to the Lord and not to men, knowing that from the Lord you will receive the reward of the inheritance; for you serve the Lord Christ.
>
> —COLOSSIANS 3:23–24

CALLED AND ACCOUNTABLE

Such incredible truth causes the Christian to pursue eternity, using time as God's gift in this pursuit. Therefore, every Christian must seek to use the whole of his or her time, to fulfill the call God has placed on his or her life. God's call is His invitation to invest in eternity by making our lives available to Him when He calls and letting God work His eternal purposes through our lives...for God's glory!

God's purpose is for you to live with eternity in mind and not merely for "time."

PRAYER & APPLICATION

Think about this past week, and consider how you invested your time. Make a list of the major activities you participated in, then place check marks beside the things you did that have eternal value.

People live forever, so time invested in people has eternal significance. Ask God if He is inviting you to encourage or disciple any certain persons. Write down their names, and ask God how you can minister to them this next week.

The Call of God Requires Character

God's goal for each believer is *"to be conformed to the image of His Son"* (Romans 8:29). Image can be understood as characteristics. In other words, God is seeking to develop the character of His Son, Jesus, in each of us. As God does this in our lives, we become better instruments to be used in His kingdom work. One of the characteristics of Jesus is His faithful obedience to do all that the Father asks of Him. Note these Scriptures:

> *In the days of His flesh, when He had offered up prayers and supplications, with vehement cries and tears to Him who was able to save Him from death, and was heard because of His godly fear, though He was a Son, yet He learned obedience by the things which He suffered. And having been perfected, He became the author of eternal salvation to all who obey Him.*
>
> —Hebrews 5:7–9

> *Then Jesus answered . . . , "Most assuredly, I say to you, the Son can do nothing of Himself, but what He sees the Father do; for whatever He does, the Son also does in like manner."*
>
> —John 5:19

> *Jesus answered them and said, "My doctrine is not Mine, but His who sent Me. If anyone wants to do His will, he shall know concerning the doctrine, whether it is from God or whether I speak on My own authority. He who speaks from himself*

seeks his own glory; but He who seeks the glory of the One
who sent Him is true, and no unrighteousness is in Him."

—JOHN 7:16–18

The result of Christ's obedience was that the Father brought eternal salvation to the human race through the Son. As God's people are obedient to make their lives available to God in the same way His Son was available to Him, God will work through them to accomplish His eternal purposes. From these three passages, we see the character of our Lord clearly.

- Jesus obeyed the Father in every area of His life.
- He only did what the Father told Him to do.
- He only spoke when the Father told Him to speak.
- He only taught what the Father told Him to teach.

Remember that God desires this same obedience in your life. As we consider that God is seeking to develop in us the character of His Son, it is important to examine this key passage in Romans:

And we know that all things work together for good to those who love God, to those who are the called according to His purpose. For whom He foreknew, He also predestined to be conformed to the image of His Son, that He might be the firstborn among many brethren. Moreover whom He predestined, these He also called; whom He called, these He also justified; and whom He justified, these He also glorified.

—Romans 8:28–30

> *He calls us into a relationship with Himself, so in that relationship, we can come to know Him and experience His working in us and through us.*

This truth carries with it much of the "why" of our being called of God. Such character is developed through our relationship with Him as He works out, in our lives, His eternal plan of redemption. He calls us into a relationship with Himself, so in that relationship, we can come to know Him and experience His working in us and through us. In that relationship, and only there, does He develop character in us in preparation for an eternity with Him.

Conformed to the Image of Christ

The entire process of developing Christlike character in every believer begins when God calls us to Himself in a relationship of love. He first redeems us from our sin, forgiving us and cleansing us and setting us apart for Himself. He places His Son in us (Colossians 1:27–29), and His Son begins to live out His life in us (Galatians 2:20), until each believer is *"perfect* [complete] *in Christ"* (Colossians 1:28).

*To them God willed to make known what are the riches of the glory of this mystery among the Gentiles: which is **Christ in you**, the hope of glory. Him we preach, warning every man and teaching every man in all wisdom, that we may present every man **perfect in Christ Jesus**. To this end I also labor, striving according to His working which works in me mightily.*

—Colossians 1:27–29 (bold added)

*I have been crucified with Christ; **it is no longer I who live, but Christ lives in me;** and the life which I now live in the flesh I live by faith in the Son of God, who loved me and gave Himself for me.*

—Galatians 2:20 (bold added)

Paul told the Galatians that he would labor with God tirelessly on their behalf until Christ be formed in them: "My little children, . . . I labor in birth again until Christ is formed in you" (Galatians 4:19).

The relationship of love that God initiates in believers continues throughout the rest of their lives. God develops us, equips us, and takes us on mission with Himself into our world. God is not willing that any should perish—in any generation or in any part of the world.

Throughout the Bible, God called many persons to Himself. We could study any one of these persons and see the eternal purpose of God unfolding. The disciples whom Jesus called to

Himself provide a clear example. As Jesus called His disciples, He said, "Follow Me." And they immediately left all and followed Him.

First, Jesus knew that each had been given to Him by the Father. As He prayed in the Garden of Gethsemane at the close of His physical life on earth, He affirmed it this way:

> *"I have manifested Your name **to the men whom You have given Me** out of the world. **They were Yours, You gave them to Me**, and they have kept Your word. Now they have known that all things which You have given Me are from You. For I have given to them the words which You have given Me; and they have received them, and have known surely that I came forth from You; and they have believed that You sent Me."*
>
> —JOHN 17:6–8 (BOLD ADDED)

Second, Jesus knew absolutely that one of His assignments from the Father was to prepare these believers for the Father's eternal purpose. That purpose was for the good news of His great salvation to be taken to the ends of the earth. Fulfillment of this purpose would occur after Jesus completed a previous critical assignment—reconciling the world to God through the Cross, the Resurrection, and the Ascension.

For the entire three and one-half years of Jesus's ministry, this is what He did—prepared the disciples. He took them with Him as He taught, preached, and healed. He revealed to them the Father and the Father's purposes—and the disciples believed. As Jesus returned to the Father, He sent the disciples into the world in the same way the Father had sent Him into the world (John 17:18; John 20:21). The *"keys of the kingdom of heaven"* were in their hands (Matthew 16:19). They would be working with the Father and the Son, in the power of the Holy Spirit, to fulfill the Father's purpose to redeem a lost world to Himself.

This was the Father's way and is still the Father's way in each of our lives when we believe in His Son, Jesus Christ. The Father calls us to His Son and gives us to Him. Jesus is still entrusted with receiving us from the Father and giving us eternal life (John 17:2–3). He continues teaching and guiding each believer, molding the believer as the Father has instructed Him until each knows the Father and responds to Him. Just as the early disciples experienced a relationship with Him by responding to His call immediately and totally, the more fully one responds, the more God uses that individual to go with Him and His risen Son on a redemptive mission to the ends of the earth. As the disciples obeyed the Lord in this relationship of love, God turned their world upside down (Acts 17:6). All through history, God has continued to do this, and He desires once again in our generation to do this same work of love.

Remember that God reveals His purposes to work through those He calls, and He is doing this in your life also. You have been given to His Son, and His Son knows what the Father has in mind for your life—in your world.

PRAYER & APPLICATION

Think back over the last few years of your life. Can you see how God has shaped your character in the past for an assignment He gave you recently?

CALLED, BECAUSE HE LOVES US!

In the mind and heart of God, so much is at stake when He calls a person! His call to us is not merely so we can go to heaven when we die, but so we can begin knowing Him, walking with Him, and serving Him from the time of salvation on and throughout eternity. He desires a relationship with those He calls—a love relationship! Jesus is the pattern of love for us. He first loved us, drew us to Himself, adopted us into His family through salvation, and sent the Holy Spirit to reside in us so that we could experience and share His love with others. Jesus describes His love for us plainly in John 15:

9 *"As the Father loved Me, I also have loved you; abide in My love.*

10 *"If you keep My commandments, you will abide in My love, just as I have kept My Father's commandments and abide in His love.*

11 *"These things I have spoken to you, that My joy may remain in you, and that your joy may be full.*

12 *"This is My commandment, that you love one another as I have loved you.*

13 *"Greater love has no one than this, than to lay down one's life for his friends.*

14 *"You are My friends if you do whatever I command you.*

15 *"No longer do I call you servants, for a servant does not know what his master is doing; but I have called you friends, for all things that I heard from My Father I have made known to you.*

16 *"You did not choose Me, but I chose you and appointed you that you should go and bear fruit, and that your fruit should remain, that whatever you ask the Father in My name He may give you.*

17 *"These things I command you, that you love one another."*

—JOHN 15:9–17

Jesus said that He loved us in the same way the Father loved Him (v. 9). He tells the disciples to *abide* in His love (v. 9). How can we abide in His love? In John 15:1–8, Jesus paints a picture showing that He is the vine and we are the branches. Sometimes we may imagine the vine as nothing more than the stem, but the vine encompasses the roots, stem, branches, leaves, and fruit. The vine is everything. The Apostle Paul describes this abiding as being *"in Christ"* and that is why he could say *"to live is Christ"* (Philippians 1:21). To abide in Him is to release your life to Him so that He can shape and transform each area of your life. To abide in His love is to let the relationship of love permeate every aspect of your life. This love relationship will grow as you read and live out the Scriptures, spend time in prayer, grow in fellowship with other Christians, and join God in service and ministry.

The evidence that we are abiding in His love is that we find ourselves obeying His commands.

The evidence that we are abiding in His love is that we find ourselves obeying His commands (John 15:10). This is not referring to a legalistic or harsh obedience, but a natural desire to follow and obey our Lord's commands out of love. Jesus tells us that as we obey Him from this love relationship, the result will be that we remain in His love in the same way that He remains in the heavenly Father's love. He goes further to explain that if we do these things, His joy will remain in us to its fullest capacity (v. 11). When we obey Him, we will abide in His love, and we will experience His joy to the fullest measure.

Jesus describes a new relationship He develops with His disciples as they learn to obey. Did you notice how Jesus described this new love relationship? Jesus says that the ones who keep His commandments will no longer be called His servants or slaves, but they will be called His friends (vv. 14–15). He goes on to describe this intimate friendship by telling the disciples that He reveals all things that He hears from His Father to the one who abides in His love (v. 15).

Let us illustrate the difference between surface knowledge of someone and abiding in that person's love. A few years ago, our family had a reunion in England. While we were there, we were able to tour Buckingham Palace and Windsor Castle. As we walked through the queen's residences, we spoke with those who worked there. They told us many things about the queen that we didn't know. As we saw the beautiful rooms and read about all of the history that had taken place in each room, we were filled with excitement. We learned a lot about the queen from those who worked for her. They *knew* her because they were with her each day; they served her. But they didn't know her like her children knew her. Her children knew her intimately and in ways that her workers would never know her.

As children of God, we have the wonderful privilege of *knowing* the King of kings intimately. We can sit at His table and listen to Him each moment. We have access to His understanding and His wisdom.

He chose us because He loved us! As we abide in Jesus's love, His love permeates all aspects of our lives and begins to flow out to others.

Jesus said to him, "'You shall love the LORD your God with all your heart, with all your soul, and with all your mind.' This is the first and great commandment. And the second is like it: 'You shall love your neighbor as yourself.' On these two commandments hang all the Law and the Prophets."

—MATTHEW 22:37–40

"A new commandment I give to you, that you love one another; as I have loved you, that you also love one another. By this all will know that you are My disciples, if you have love for one another."

—JOHN 13:34–35

But concerning brotherly love you have no need that I should write to you, for you yourselves are taught by God to love one another; and indeed you do so toward all the brethren who are in all Macedonia. But we urge you, brethren, that you increase more and more; that you also aspire to lead a quiet life, to mind your own business, and to work with your own hands, as we commanded you, that you may walk properly toward those who are outside, and that you may lack nothing.

—1 THESSALONIANS 4:9–12

Prayer & Application

Think back over the last few weeks or months. Would you (or someone close to you) be able to describe your life as a life that abides in love? Have your recent actions and attitudes toward those you relate to daily (your spouse, your children, your neighbors, your co-workers, and your church family) been expressed in love?

Prayerfully commit your heart to abide in the love of Christ Jesus, and ask God to enable His love to be expressed through all of your relationships.

Count Nicholas Ludwig von Zinzendorf

"All this have I done for you. What are you doing for Me?"

Nicholas Ludwig von Zinzendorf was born in 1700 in Dresden, Germany, into one of the noblest families of Europe. As a young adult, Nicholas visited an art museum in Düsseldorf, Germany, where he saw the painting by Domenico Feti titled *Ecce Homo* (*Behold the Man*). The painting depicted Christ with a crown of thorns on His head and the legend, "All this have I done for you. What are you doing for Me?" The face of Christ in the painting never left Zinzendorf's heart, and Christ's love became the compelling force of his life.

The love Zinzendorf felt for his Savior expressed itself in his love for other believers, especially through a small group of approximately 300 Moravians whom he allowed to establish a church on his estate at Herrnhut in 1722. He helped the Moravians develop a deep passion for their Savior and helped them to live out Christ's command to love one another.

Zinzendorf's love for Christ was also expressed through his life of prayer. He spent countless hours in communion with his Savior and sought to lead others to commit to a life of prayer. His example led the Moravian believers to begin a powerful prayer movement they called "hourly intercession." They prayed in shifts, 24 hours a day, 7 days a week, for the work of

Christ around the world. This "hourly intercession" went on uninterrupted for more than 100 years!

The desire Zinzendorf had to reach those who did not know his Savior was another manifestation of his passion for Jesus. By 1752, the Moravian Church at Herrnhut had sent out more missionaries than the whole Protestant church had done in 200 years. Before long, they had three members on the missions field for every one at their church in Herrnhut. All of this was accomplished by men and women with little formal and theological education, but with a burning passion for their Savior, Jesus Christ.

Zinzendorf's life was a labor of love for his Savior, who had done so much for him and a lost and dying world.

CHAPTER 2

What Is a Call?

ESSENTIAL TRUTH

One must believe that God really does speak to us in this matter of His call. From Genesis through Revelation, no truth stands out any clearer than that *God speaks to His people*. They always know that it is God, they know what He is saying, and they know how they are to respond. In other words, this is not just an academic exercise or merely a theological truth. It is a real relationship with God, and He really does call each of us to Himself for His eternal purposes. This truth is foundational to our study of being called and accountable!

> *"And this is eternal life, that they may know You, the only true God, and Jesus Christ whom You have sent."*
>
> —JOHN 17:3

Judith Tunell

God Gave Her a New Assignment

Judith was a paralegal. One day, while she was pregnant with her second child and driving to the law firm where she worked, she was suddenly struck with blindness. She then began to experience many physical problems that affected her hearing and her ability to walk. This all happened within a 24-hour period. In one day, she lost her ability to work, her independence, her ability to see, and her ability to hear. This experience served as a wake-up call to Judith, showing her that God had a new direction for her life. God used these dramatic circumstances to bring her into a new realm in her relationship with Him.

As Judith began to adjust to being legally blind and to her significant loss of hearing, she realized for the first time what it was like to be disabled. God gave her a desire to minister to people with disabilities and made her aware of the day-to-day difficulties they encounter in society. She became an encourager to the discouraged as she began to get involved in her city government as an advocate for the disabled. Judith is very articulate and kind, and God gave her the words to speak to the city officials regarding some of the basic needs of the disabled. As a result of her obedience, the city of Phoenix made radical changes throughout the city to accommodate the disabled. Looking back, she says that "God's assignment was for her to put a face with a problem and to stand before the leaders to hold them accountable." She dealt with them as a Christian; she honored her Lord and He honored her. She built relationships with government leaders, became a friend to many on the city council, and has been appointed to leadership roles on several boards relating to the disabled. She always knew that God had a plan for her life and her disabilities, but she had never really internalized what that meant.

As she sought to study God's Word and to take part in Bible studies with other believers, she realized that there were very few Christian resources for the legally blind. Thus, God has given her a new assignment: to work with Christian publishers so they can make discipleship material available for the disabled. Judith could not read regular-sized print in books, so she often asked a friend to read to her. "Nothing was available in a format that I could read," she said. Through many different circumstances, Judith is currently working with some people from the Christian Booksellers Association in hopes of making Christian publishers aware of the needs of the disabled regarding discipleship material. Recently, Judith, with the help of two friends, translated *Experiencing God: Knowing and Doing the Will of God* into a format that could be printed in Braille. Judith cultivated a partnership with two publishers, through whom Braille copies of *Experiencing God* are now readily available for the blind.* God has used Judith's life to minister to and encourage thousands of people with disabilities. An ordinary person called by God is doing extraordinary works!

*If interested in obtaining a copy of the *Experiencing God* workbook in Braille, contact the Assemblies of God Center for the Blind. Write or email Caryl Weingartner or Paul Weingartner, Assemblies of God, National Center for the Blind, 1445 N. Boonville Ave., Springfield, MO 65802; (417) 831-1964; fax (417) 862-5120, or email *Blind@ag.org*.

A Call to Relationship

From the very beginning in the Garden of Eden, we see God bringing Adam and Eve into being and "calling" them to Himself.

> *Then the LORD God called to Adam and said to him, "Where are you?"*
> —GENESIS 3:9

It was preeminently a call to a love relationship with God. God created them in His love. He instructed Adam (and later, Eve) to partner with Him by naming the animals and by having dominion over all God had created (Genesis 1:28). God continued to give Adam and Eve instructions about the stewardship and accountability of their assignments. The character of God's perfect creation is found in the repetitive words, *"God said," "and it was so,"* and *"it was good."*

It was good. This was supremely true about God's relationship of love with Adam and Eve. This is always true with God when He brings any person into His world!

But sin entered into the lives of Adam and Eve, and the loving relationship with God was broken. Reading again the pitiful picture of Adam and Eve hiding themselves from the presence of God and then the heart cry of God to Adam, *"Where are you?"* (Genesis 3:8–10) can cause one to weep. Adam and Eve were afraid of God. What a change in relationship!

Disobedience separates us from God. We must return to God through repentance of sin in order to keep our fellowship with the Father unhindered.

When our youngest child became a Christian, God taught our family a very special lesson about the relationship He desires to have with His people. Our daughter had been asking about becoming a Christian for months. I remember so well the day that God saved her! She became a Christian during our breakfast-time devotion. As my wife, Dana, walked with our young daughter throughout that day, they talked about her being a Christian and what God had done in her life. Later in the day, our daughter and son had a disagreement. Dana reminded them that they were both Christians and began to correct their wrong behavior. Before she was finished, our daughter announced, "I don't feel like a Christian!" Dana responded, "The reason you don't feel like a Christian is because you have sinned and need to ask Jesus to forgive you for how you just treated your brother." A few minutes later our daughter came to Dana and said, "You're right, Mom. I asked Jesus to forgive me, and now I feel like a Christian again." The love relationship had been severed through sin, and once our daughter repented of her sin, the relationship was immediately restored. This example serves as a simple picture of how quickly we can allow our hearts to turn away from the love relationship with our Lord and how quickly that relationship can be restored through repentance.

When we sin, we too might want to hide from the Lord, as did Adam and Eve, or maybe we simply don't "feel like a Christian" afterward. However, we must be quick to learn that it is our sin that causes separation in this love relationship, and we must humble ourselves and return to the Lord in repentance to have the fellowship restored.

> *The Bible is the story of God's redemptive love providing everyone who will believe in Him a way back to His love.*

Throughout all generations, God has called His people to return to a love relationship with Him. The Bible is the story of God's redemptive love providing everyone who will believe in Him a way back to His love. God gave salvation through His Son so that His eternal purpose of love could be restored.

Too often, people think of this salvation as simply providing a way to go to heaven at death, which is certainly a vital part of God's great salvation. However, as we have noted, God did not create us for time, but for eternity! It is important at this point in our study to keep in mind Jesus's definition of "eternal life":

> *"And this is eternal life, that they may know You, the only true God, and Jesus Christ whom You have sent."*
>
> —JOHN 17:3

Did you notice the key phrase in Jesus's definition of eternal life? The key phrase is *"they may know You."*

The phrase *to know* carries with it a huge meaning. *The Amplified Bible* helps us understand the definition more thoroughly. For example, in John 17:3 and Philippians 3:10, *The Amplified Bible* describes eternal life and what it means "to know" God the Father and Son.

> "And this is eternal life: [it means] to know (to perceive, recognize, become acquainted with, and understand) You, the only true and real God, and [likewise] to know Him, Jesus [as the] Christ (the Anointed One, the Messiah), Whom You have sent."
>
> —JOHN 17:3 (AMP)

> [For my determined purpose is] that I may know Him [that I may progressively become more deeply and intimately acquainted with Him, perceiving and recognizing and understanding the wonders of His Person more strongly and more clearly], and that I may in that same way come to know the power outflowing from His resurrection [which it exerts over believers], and that I may so share His sufferings as to be continually transformed [in spirit into His likeness even] to His death.
>
> —PHILIPPIANS 3:10 (AMP)

If we were to rephrase these verses in our own words, we could say: "Eternal life begins when we come to know Jesus Christ as our Savior. At that point, life on earth becomes the opportunity to be increasingly more intimately acquainted with Him each day. Our life purpose is set: to become more and more deeply familiar with Him and His ways."

Thus God's call is to His great salvation, provided in His Son, and is an incredible expression of His eternal love for each of us. You catch the enormous nature of this relationship as the Apostle Paul bears witness to his new "life in Christ."

Let's take a moment to examine how Paul describes his life in Christ. In the following Scriptures, notice how Paul describes his own personal love relationship with Jesus Christ.

> *But by the grace of God I am what I am, and His grace toward me was not in vain; but I labored more abundantly than they all, yet not I, but the grace of God which was with me.*
>
> —1 CORINTHIANS 15:10

> *"For I through the law died to the law that I might live to God. I have been crucified with Christ; it is no longer I who live, but Christ lives in me; and the life which I now live in the flesh I live by faith in the Son of God, who loved me and gave Himself for me."*
>
> —GALATIANS 2:19–20

> *For me to live is Christ [His life in me], and to die is gain [the gain of the glory of eternity].*
>
> —PHILIPPIANS 1:21 (AMP)

*I have strength for all things in Christ Who empowers me
[I am ready for anything and equal to anything through Him
Who infuses inner strength into me; I am self-sufficient in
Christ's sufficiency].*

—PHILIPPIANS 4:13 (AMP)

Paul realized that all of his accomplishments and all of the incredible miracles that God had done through his life were a direct result of God's grace—His unmerited favor and blessing. He had come to the end of himself and had learned to let the Holy Spirit live unhindered through him. As he discusses the possibility of dying, he describes it as *"gain"* because he had come to know and experience the personal relationship of Christ living out His life in him. Paul knew that the power and strength for his work came through his fellowship with Christ.

All of Paul's letters are full of such expressions of love to his Lord. He speaks out of his personal experience when he urges every believer to *"be filled with the Spirit"* (Ephesians 5:18) and to *"be filled with all the fullness of God"* (Ephesians 3:19).

In John 15, Jesus describes vividly life in Him. Take a moment to read the following passage and pay careful attention to how Jesus describes His relationship to the Father and how we are to relate to the Son:

"I am the true vine, and My Father is the vinedresser. Every branch in Me that does not bear fruit He takes away; and every branch that bears fruit He prunes, that it may bear more fruit. You are already clean because of the word which I have spoken to you. Abide in Me, and I in you. As the branch cannot bear fruit of itself, unless it abides in the vine, neither can you, unless you abide in Me. I am the vine, you are the branches. He who abides in Me, and I in him, bears much fruit; for without Me you can do nothing. If anyone does not abide in Me, he is cast out as a branch and is withered; and they gather them and throw them into the fire, and they are burned. If you abide in Me, and My words abide in you, you will ask what you desire, and it shall be done for you. By this My Father is glorified, that you bear much fruit; so you will be My disciples. As the Father loved Me, I also have loved you; abide in My love. If you keep My commandments, you will abide in My love, just as I have kept My Father's commandments and abide in His love. These things I have spoken to you, that My joy may remain in you, and that your joy may be full."

—JOHN 15:1–11

Jesus said that He is the Vine and we are the branches and that we can do nothing without Him. If persons close to you (spouse, co-worker, pastor, friend) were to describe your life in Christ, how would they describe it? Would they say, "Without God, he [or she] can do nothing?" Or would they say, "Without God, she [or he] cannot do very much?" Maybe they would describe your life like this, "Without God, he [or she] can do most things."

If God were to describe your life in Christ, how would He describe it?

When you read the testimonies of those in the Bible and in history who have described their relationship with God, they usually tell of the overwhelming *relationship of love* that took place when they were called of God.

This call of God is to every believer. The essence of the call is to an intimate and life-giving relationship with God, which is totally life transforming and ultimately world changing.

PRAYER & APPLICATION

How has God's love transformed your life since you came into an intimate relationship with Christ? Spend some time thanking God for this transformation and asking Him to open you to any further change He wants to bring to your life.

GOD INITIATES THE CALL

In this entire process, God takes the initiative to come to His people and to let them know what He is doing or about to do. He came to Noah at the moment He was about to judge the world by a flood. Unless God had come to him, Noah could not have known what was about to happen. But Noah did know because God wanted to accomplish His purpose through Noah. So God gave Noah an assignment, and Noah responded as a co-worker with God.

When God was about to free His people from slavery in Egypt, He took the initiative to come to Moses and let Moses know what He was about to do. This revelation was God's invitation for Moses to work with Him to accomplish His purposes for His people. God came this way to each of the prophets.

Let's take a moment to look at the following Scriptures and notice how God initiated the *relationship* and the *call* of these individuals.

THE CALL OF SIMON PETER, JAMES, AND JOHN

So it was, as the multitude pressed about Him to hear the word of God, that He stood by the Lake of Gennesaret, and saw two boats standing by the lake; but the fishermen had gone from them and were washing their nets. Then He got into one of the boats, which was Simon's, and asked him to put out a little from the land. And He sat down and taught the multitudes from the boat. When He had stopped speaking, He said to Simon, "Launch out into the deep and let down your nets for a catch." But Simon answered and said to Him, "Master, we have toiled all night and caught nothing; nevertheless at Your word I will let down the net." And when they had done this, they caught a great number of fish, and their net was breaking. So they signaled to their partners in the other boat to come and help them. And they came and filled both the boats, so that they began to sink. When Simon Peter saw it, he fell down at Jesus' knees, saying, "Depart from me, for I am a sinful man, O Lord!" For he and all who were with him were astonished at the catch of fish which they had taken; and so also were James and John, the sons of Zebedee, who were partners with Simon. And Jesus said to Simon, "Do not be afraid. From now on you will catch men." So when they had brought their boats to land, they forsook all and followed Him.

—LUKE 5:1–11

THE CALL OF MATTHEW

As Jesus passed on from there, He saw a man named Matthew sitting at the tax office. And He said to him, "Follow Me." So he arose and followed Him.

—MATTHEW 9:9

THE CALL OF JEREMIAH

Then the word of the LORD came to me, saying:
"Before I formed you in the womb I knew you;
Before you were born I sanctified you;
I ordained you a prophet to the nations."
Then said I:
"Ah, Lord GOD!
Behold, I cannot speak, for I am a youth."
But the LORD said to me:

"Do not say, 'I am a youth,'
For you shall go to all to whom I send you,
And whatever I command you, you shall speak.
Do not be afraid of their faces,
For I am with you to deliver you," says the LORD.
Then the LORD put forth His hand and touched my mouth,
and the LORD said to me:
"Behold, I have put My words in your mouth.
See, I have this day set you over the nations and over
the kingdoms,
To root out and to pull down,
To destroy and to throw down,
To build and to plant."

—JEREMIAH 1:4–10

THE CALL OF JONAH

Now the word of the LORD came to Jonah the son of Amittai,
saying, "Arise, go to Nineveh, that great city, and cry out
against it; for their wickedness has come up before Me."

—JONAH 1:1–2

Can you see from these examples that God takes the initiative?
God encountered each person right in the middle of his daily
routine, brought him to Himself, and then used the person
to accomplish His work. In the cases of Peter, James, John,
and Matthew, we see them immediately forsake all and follow Him. They were not given specific instruction as to what

they would be doing, except to join the Lord. Jeremiah and Jonah were given more details as to what God had in mind for their lives.

Jeremiah was given the difficult assignment to deliver an unpopular message to the people of Judah. The people of Jeremiah's day had continually rejected God's commands as well as the words from His prophets. Jeremiah's ministry would reveal the hardness of heart of the people, and the prophet would face much ridicule and hardship to live out the call of God upon his life. God knew what Jeremiah would face as he lived out this assignment, and that is why you see the strong words and details that were given to the prophet. God took the initiative to call Jeremiah, but also provided him with the message and the assurance to live out the call.

Jonah is not the best example of how to respond to God coming to our lives to give us an assignment. However, it seems that many of God's people respond more like Jonah than the other examples. Again, God took the initiative, came to Jonah, and gave him the assignment. God knew all that was needed for the people of Nineveh to repent was for Jonah to deliver the message. God knew what their hearts were like and knew what their response would be. When you look at all of the examples here, looking back, Jonah had the easiest assignment. Jeremiah would be called the weeping prophet from the burden of the message and the hardships he experienced. The disciples would face all kinds of hardships and persecution. Jonah was asked to deliver a word from God to a people who were ready to repent. However, Jonah did not respond to God's initiative because his heart was not willing to let go of personal prejudices and pride. We can look back now and see how simple it would have been if he had the obedient heart of Matthew.

To the disciples, Jesus said, *"You did not choose Me, but I chose you and appointed you that you should go and bear fruit, and that your fruit should remain, that whatever you ask the Father in My name He may give you"* (John 15:16). Throughout history, this pattern is seen every time God was about to do a great work in our world, and it is still the pattern used today. This is true right now for your life also! He chose you.

God chooses us so that our lives will bear fruit. At times, it may be hard to understand what "fruit" looks like in our lives. Certainly a good place to start would be Galatians 5:22–23: *"But the fruit of the Spirit is love, joy, peace, longsuffering, kindness, goodness, faithfulness, gentleness, self-control."* As God calls you and begins to work in your life so that He can use you, you should see these characteristics growing in your life.

Our lives should be producing other kinds of fruit along with those listed in Galatians. For example, in Colossians 1:10, Paul describes the fruit of good works and growing *"in the knowledge of God"*; and in Philippians 1:11 (AMP), he describes a fruit that is abounding in "*right standing with God and right doing*," which glorifies God. James portrays a wisdom fruit that is "*pure, then peaceable, gentle, willing to yield, full of mercy and good fruits, without partiality and without hypocrisy.*" He goes on to say that peaceful people bear *righteousness* as fruit (James 3:17–18).

When God chose us, He also designed our lives to bear good fruit. This fruit includes our character as well as our service to God in His work. With the strong emphasis that Jesus placed on bearing fruit (Luke 13:6–9), it is important to look and see what your life is yielding.

Prayer & Application

Take some time to evaluate your life to see if these characteristics (the fruit of the Spirit) are "growing" in your life. Write in your spiritual journal which ones are evident in your life and which ones are not. Ask God what changes He wants to bring into your life in regard to your findings.

Obeying the Call Requires Adjustments

The call of God will always involve some kind of major adjustment in your life to be the person God can use to accomplish His purposes. Moses had to leave herding sheep to lead

God's people. David could not be a shepherd and be king at the same time. The disciples of Jesus could not continue their fishing and follow Jesus to learn to become fishers of men.

When lawyers, doctors, schoolteachers, truck drivers, salespeople, nurses, or bankers become Christians, they respond to Christ as Lord over all of their lives, so He can accomplish His plans through His people. God may leave Christians in their present vocations or professional positions. However, when He does, it will not be "business as usual" or business as the world around them would have it. They will thoroughly realize that they have been *"bought at a price,"* and, therefore, they are, at all times and in all places, to make sure they glorify God in their bodies and in their spirits, which are His (1 Corinthians 6:19–20). Since God dwells fully within them, every place they put their feet is holy ground, for God is present in them. That makes the workplace a place where God can accomplish His eternal purposes through them, right there! The classroom becomes a "workplace for God" for one called to be a teacher or student. The garage is God's place of evangelism and discipleship for a car mechanic. The doctor's office or surgery suite becomes God's workplace for a medical doctor or nurse; the lawyer's office or courtroom, for the lawyer or judge; and the halls of government, for the congressman, mayor, or political

The arena of activity God chooses for each believer is entirely up to God.

official. But the choice, the arena of activity God chooses for each believer, is entirely up to God.

One of the greatest developments today is the tremendous number of missions volunteers who are leaving all and following Jesus—across North America and around the world. Teachers are going into China so our Lord can reach Chinese people through them. Businesspeople are making their lives available through their business connections around the world so Christ can bring to Himself lost persons who would not hear any other way. Tens of thousands of volunteers are going around the world each year with a deep sense of being on mission with their Lord. What a difference this is making in our generation!

FROM NORMAN: EXPERIENCING GOD AT WORK ON THE RAILROAD
My wife, Dana, worked for a railroad for several years while I was in seminary. Her responsibilities changed as the railroad she worked for merged with another railroad. She was moved into a new position in which she managed the severance packages for both companies. God put her in that position and used her to touch many people who were losing their jobs.

One person affected by the layoffs was a Christian woman whom God used in a very special way to touch the people of India. As she had the opportunity to get to know my wife, she shared with Dana a burden God had laid on her heart to send *Experiencing God* to her denominational missionaries in India. There she was with a burden to get *Experiencing God* to the missionaries without any idea how to do it. In the process of working through her severance package, she was introduced to the author's daughter-in-law. God had more than severance packages in mind when He placed Dana in that position.

She and Dana worked on the project together, and God led them to a printer who would print the book in the language of preference for each of the missionaries. More than 5,000 copies of *Experiencing God* were provided to these missionaries. God used a woman who lost her job to bring the message of knowing God and doing His will to thousands of people in India. When believers make themselves available to God, He can and will complete His work through them. This is a prime example of allowing God to work all things together for good in those who are called and accountable!

If believers were to think carefully about their present relationship with God, they would realize that the greatest challenge is not that they do not know the will of God, but rather that they do know His will but have not been willing to obey Him! Neither God nor history waits on believers' responses to God's call and claim on their lives.

God's call requires only one response from every believer—obedience! Once you, as a child of God, recognize the activity of God in your life, you must immediately, without resistance or discussion, respond obediently to all God is directing. Only then will you experience God's working mightily through your life. At times, we tend to take our obedience to God lightly. However, God views our obedience as an essential key to our relationship with Him.

Let's look at a few examples in the Scriptures. As you read these verses, pay careful attention to how God views our obedience or disobedience to Him.

"If you love Me, keep My commandments."

—JOHN 14:15

Jesus answered and said to him, "If anyone loves Me, he will keep My word; and My Father will love him, and We will come to him and make Our home with him. He who does not love Me does not keep My words; and the word which you hear is not Mine but the Father's who sent Me."

—JOHN 14:23–24

So Samuel said: "Has the LORD as great delight in burnt offerings and sacrifices, as in obeying the voice of the LORD? Behold, to obey is better than sacrifice, and to heed than the fat of rams."

—1 SAMUEL 15:22

Jesus's love for us was settled on the Cross. Our love for Jesus is expressed daily through our obedience to Him.

The Father sees our love for Him when we have an obedient heart. This was true in the life of Hudson Taylor. He was training as a medical doctor when God made it unmistakably clear that He wanted to reach the peoples of inland China with the gospel through Taylor's life. Hudson Taylor was obedient, and God did reach hundreds of thousands, even millions, of precious Chinese people through his life and those God would bring alongside him to preach, teach, and heal in China.

Jesus's love for us was settled on the Cross. Our love for Jesus is expressed daily through our obedience to Him.

Further, a call from God always involves the person in the corporate life of the people of God. Even God's call to Abram involved all the people of God who would follow Abram. God's call to Moses directly involved God's purposes in the lives of His chosen people. God's call to Joshua, the judges, Samuel, David, the prophets, the disciples, and Paul brought them into the midst of what God had purposed to do through their lives as His people and for others He was calling.

In the New Testament, the redemptive work of God was to be through the life of His people functioning together in local churches. Through these churches, God would take His great salvation to the ends of the earth, even to every

CALLED AND ACCOUNTABLE

person. Every believer should anticipate God involving them dynamically in their local church. God will then, as He did in the New Testament times, involve each church in the lives of sister churches that He has established in His kingdom. This will involve linking with churches of other denominations as well.

Obedience is always the key to experiencing a life on mission with God in our world!

PRAYER & APPLICATION

Spend some time in prayer asking God to show you how He is working through your life where He has placed you.

As you prayed, did God show you any adjustments He is asking you to make today? Is there any area of your life in which God is clearly inviting you to follow Him, but you have not yet responded? If so, respond to Him now.

THE CALL IS REDEMPTIVE

Another aspect of this relationship and calling that is so often overlooked or neglected is that this relationship is always redemptive! This means the call to salvation is, at the same time, a call to be on mission with God to reach the lost in the world. The moment individuals are brought into relation-ship with God, they experience the heart of God, the mind of God, and the eternal purposes of God. All that is on the heart of Jesus, who now dwells within them through the Holy Spirit, increasingly becomes a part of their hearts (John 16:12–15). It is impossible to live intimately with God and not be *"transformed into the same image from glory to glory, just as by the Spirit of the Lord"* (2 Corinthians 3:18).

From the moment of salvation, there comes over the new believer a deep sense of being on mission with the Lord in their world.

As God transforms us, He lays His heart over ours, and we begin to share His burden—that He is *"not willing that any should perish but that all should come to repentance"* (2 Peter 3:9). God, who sent His only Son into the world that we, through Him, might be saved (John 3:16), will also send us into the world that others might be saved by our witness to His great salvation.

This truth, again, is seen throughout the entire Bible, and all those mightily used throughout history bear witness to its reality. From the moment of salvation, there comes over the new believer a deep sense of being on mission with the Lord in their world. Some indicate that, at salvation, they sensed a call to missions, evangelism, and/or witnessing. This is normal for every new believer.

Let me illustrate this process from the life of a friend named John, who was working as a personal bodyguard for a member of a high-profile family in Texas. Earlier in John's life, he had sensed a call to missions and ministry, but through the years, he had wandered away from the Lord and was not serving as God had intended. Through circumstances out of John's control, he was falsely accused of some things and demoted to sitting in a guard shack outside of one of the family's homes. During this time, he had the option to become angry but, instead, looked to God for understanding. God assured John that the call to be on mission with Him had not changed after all of the wasted years. John released his life to the Lord and renewed his commitment to the call. Within a short time, a ministry contacted John to serve by working with boys and men. Today, John travels the country working with churches and associations of churches, calling men back to their relationship to God. To talk with him is to hear a heart that loves to serve the Lord and help men and boys encounter God through many different venues. To look over his life is to see that God had never released him from the call and was working in his life to cause him to will and want to follow God's claim on his life.

In Philippians 2:5–11, Paul urged the believers in the church at Philippi to accept the mind of Christ—*"Let this mind be in you which was also in Christ Jesus"* (v. 5)—and then identified what this would mean specifically. He expected the mind of Christ to be formed in them, so he urged them to let it happen. Then he added,

> *Work out your own salvation with fear and trembling; for it is God who works in you both to will and to do for His good pleasure.*
>
> —PHILIPPIANS 2:12–13

> *Now may the God of peace who brought up our Lord Jesus from the dead, that great Shepherd of the sheep, through the blood of the everlasting covenant, make you complete in every good work to do His will, working in you what is well pleasing in His sight, through Jesus Christ, to whom be glory forever and ever. Amen.*
>
> —HEBREWS 13:20–21

In Hebrews 13:20–21, we read that God desires to equip and enable you with everything you need for doing His will. What God meant was that each believer must let the full implications of salvation work into every area of life. Each Christian must respond to Him as Lord over all of his or her life, for it is now He who will be working in the life of the believer, causing that person to want to do His will, and then working in that life to enable the person to do it. What an exciting invitation for every believer!

My own Christian life began with a deep sense that God had something in mind when He saved me. (*"You did not choose Me, but I chose you and appointed you that you should go and bear fruit, and that your fruit should remain"* [John 15:16].) Regardless what task God presented to me, I responded to Him as His servant. I began by leading youth. As I led the youth, I watched for anything God would desire to do through my life. Then a church asked if I would be their music/education director. It never crossed my mind not to respond, for I knew that the call to salvation was, at the same time, the call to serve with God in my world.

Two years later, that same church asked if I would be their pastor. I agreed and served for five years. After many years of pastoring, some churches asked if I would be their director of missions. I agreed and served for six years. Then the North American Mission Board (an agency of the Southern Baptist Convention) asked if I would guide our Convention toward prayer and spiritual awakening. I did that with them, as well as with the International Mission Board (another agency of the Southern Baptist Convention) and LifeWay Christian Resources, until April of 2000. Since that time, I have continued serving around the world through Blackaby Ministries International.

No matter what assignment God has given me over the past 45 years of ministry, I have always responded to Him as His servant. And He has always been faithful to equip me for whatever assignment He gives. Over these years, my focus has not been on the assignments, but to faithfully honor God in the relationship of being His servant.

PRAYER & APPLICATION

It is an awesome truth to understand that the God of the universe calls you to be on mission with Him in your world. When He calls you, He is inviting you to follow Him. Accepting His invitation requires you to make adjustments in your life.

As you look back over the past few months or years, you probably recognize many times when God invited you to be on mission with Him. What adjustments has your obedience to follow Him caused you to make? (You might think of this in terms of your family, workplace, community, or church.)

Pray and ask God to show you areas in which He is inviting you to join Him this week. What adjustments will you need to make to join Him in His activity?

A CALL TO BE ON MISSION

Every Christian is called to be on mission with God in our world. This is what it means to be called. God is seeking to bring a lost world back to Himself. He loves every person, and He is not willing that any should perish. He has always been working in our world to seek and to save those who are lost. That is what He was doing when He called you! Those He saves, He involves as fellow workers with Himself in His eternal purpose to save a lost world.

But to every sincere leader in every succeeding generation, Paul adds significantly, *"Behold, now is the accepted time; behold, now is the day of salvation"* (2 Corinthians 6:2). In other words, the moment of their call was the moment God would be at work to redeem their world. It would be God's strategic moment of favor toward the people to whom the gospel would be preached. Paul knew this in real experience, for he was living as a worker with God. He was not only invited to join God but was given the enabling grace of God to be used of God to bring multitudes to salvation.

A wonderful example of this truth is seen in the life of Joseph, the earthly father of Jesus. Let's take a moment to read from Matthew's account:

Now the birth of Jesus Christ was as follows: After His mother Mary was betrothed to Joseph, before they came together, she was found with child of the Holy Spirit. Then Joseph her husband, being a just man, and not wanting to make her a public example, was minded to put her away secretly. But while he thought about these things, behold, an angel of the Lord appeared to him in a dream, saying, "Joseph, son of David, do not be afraid to take to you Mary your wife, for that which is conceived in her is of the Holy Spirit. And she will bring forth a Son, and you shall call His name JESUS, for He will save His people from their sins." So all this was done that it might be fulfilled which was spoken by the Lord through the prophet, saying: "Behold, the virgin shall be with child, and bear a Son, and they shall call His name Immanuel," which is translated, "God with us." **Then Joseph, being aroused from sleep, did as the angel of the Lord commanded him** and took to him his wife, and did not know her till she had brought forth her firstborn Son. And he called His name JESUS.

—MATTHEW 1:18–25 (BOLD ADDED)

Now when they had departed, behold, an angel of the Lord appeared to Joseph in a dream, saying, "Arise, take the young Child and His mother, flee to Egypt, and stay there until I bring you word; for Herod will seek the young Child to destroy Him." **When he arose, he took the young Child and His mother by night and departed for Egypt,** and was there until the death of Herod, that it might be fulfilled which was spoken by the Lord through the prophet, saying, "Out of Egypt I called My Son."

—MATTHEW 2:13–15 (BOLD ADDED)

But when Herod was dead, behold, an angel of the Lord appeared in a dream to Joseph in Egypt, saying, "Arise, take the young Child and His mother, and go to the land of Israel, for those who sought the young Child's life are dead." **Then he arose, took the young Child and His mother, and came**

into the land of Israel. *But when he heard that Archelaus was reigning over Judea instead of his father Herod, he was afraid to go there. And being warned by God in a dream, he turned aside into the region of Galilee. And he came and dwelt in a city called Nazareth, that it might be fulfilled which was spoken by the prophets, "He shall be called a Nazarene."*

—MATTHEW 2:19–23 (BOLD ADDED)

What was God about to do when He came to Joseph? He was about to bring salvation to the world.

Did you notice how quickly Joseph obeyed each time God spoke to him?

Can you imagine what the outcome could have been had he not recognized God's instructions and stepped out in faith quickly?

His immediate obedience meant life or death to his family! One man's obedience fulfilled prophecy and saved the life of his child. In the same way, when God speaks to us, the timing is critical, and the lives of those closest to us may depend on our quick faith and obedience. When God gives you an assignment you can trust that His timing is perfect!

PRAYER & APPLICATION

Has God instructed you to do something recently? How did you respond? Did you recognize the importance of the timing of God's instructions as they fit into His eternal plans? Take some time now to pray and ask God if He has given you any instruction to which you have not responded.

If God brings to mind some areas in which you have not responded, write them down and ask the Lord to help you adjust your life immediately to His will.

FROM HENRY: AN EXAMPLE FROM THE CORPORATE WORLD
Immediate obedience will affect every area of your life—your family, your church, your community, and your workplace. I see this unfolding day after day in the lives of CEOs in corporate America. I have the wonderful privilege of "working" with more than 160 of these strategic men and women placed in the corporate world by God for such a time as this! God is touching their minds and hearts deeply. They have an inner sense that not only is God at work in them and around them, but that He clearly wants greater access to work His kingdom purposes through them. They are seeking the Lord with all their hearts, as God said He would cause them to do. And they are readying their lives, their marriages, their homes, and their business lives to be available to God in a maximum way. Month after month, we hear how God is using them to accomplish His purposes in our day throughout the world as they obey His commands immediately.

We are hearing this same pattern of God's activity in teenagers in their schools, in college students on their campuses, and in so many women who believe that God is about to work toward a great revival in the nation through women wholly available to God. We believe this may be a vital part of God's strategy for redeeming our world in our day.

There is a sudden and extensive move of God, causing every believer to sense that his or her life is indeed on mission with God at this time. God is truly on mission with His people in our day. There is no sense that only a few are called. All are called, and each Christian is urged to *"walk worthy of the calling"* (Ephesians 4:1).

As you read the following verses, notice how these believers are described as walking *"worthy of the calling."*

> *And you became followers of us and of the Lord, having received the word in much affliction, with joy of the Holy Spirit, so that you became examples to all in Macedonia and Achaia who believe. For from you the word of the Lord has sounded forth, not only in Macedonia and Achaia, but also in every place. Your faith toward God has gone out, so that we do not need to say anything.*
>
> —1 THESSALONIANS 1:6–8

> *I thank my God, making mention of you always in my prayers, hearing of your love and faith which you have toward the Lord Jesus and toward all the saints, that the sharing of*

your faith may become effective by the acknowledgment of every good thing which is in you in Christ Jesus. For we have great joy and consolation in your love, because the hearts of the saints have been refreshed by you, brother.

—PHILEMON 4–7

For I am already being poured out as a drink offering, and the time of my departure is at hand. I have fought the good fight, I have finished the race, I have kept the faith. Finally, there is laid up for me the crown of righteousness, which the Lord, the righteous Judge, will give to me on that Day, and not to me only but also to all who have loved His appearing.

—2 TIMOTHY 4:6–8

The people of Thessalonica received the Word and became an example to all believers in such a powerful way that Paul describes it as *"the word of the Lord has sounded forth"* from them. Philemon was known as one who refreshed the hearts of the saints. And Paul describes himself at the end of his life as having *"fought the good fight."* In addition, he realized that he was finishing the race (the calling or life assignment) God had given him.

Spend some time in the coming days asking God if your life can be described as walking *"worthy of the calling with which you were called."*

Prayer & Application

Take a moment this week to write in your spiritual journal the areas of your life that you can sense are pleasing to God, and spend time thanking God for strengthening you to honor Him.

Also, note the areas in which you recognize you have not been walking worthy of His call. Take time to repent of any sins He reveals to you, and then ask God to help you turn these areas completely over to Him.

Jim and Kaye Johns
Teaching God's People to Pray

Jim and Kaye Johns direct PrayerPower, a ministry "to help God's people learn to pray." They began this ministry in response to a clear call from God when Kaye was 52 years old and Jim was 62.

For years, Jim had owned an advertising agency and managed several radio stations. He also did radio program syndication and marketing consulting. Kaye, on the other hand, because of a handicapped daughter, developed and ran a center for successful learning, where she taught schoolteachers how to teach children with special learning needs.

But God rearranged their lives when they went through a course on prayer life taught by T. W. Hunt. Later they were deeply affected by their study of *Experiencing God*, which they taught to more than 1,000 people over the next three years. In 1994, they clearly knew that "God had another plan" for them. They realized God was initiating a life-changing direction for their family. They began to experience a "whole new life," as they were called to a prayer ministry.

As time has passed, they have been invited to churches all over the world to teach multitudes of people. They said, "God gathered up everything we had ever done, and directed us to encourage and teach God's people to pray." This now has led them to producing a video series teaching prayer and eight booklets on prayer for many aspects of the life of God's people.

They now see clearly that God called them, ordinary people in their later years, to an enormous new relationship with Him. He is using them to teach His people to pray, and, in turn, God is touching multitudes and drawing many to Himself. They not only have been called, they have been accountable to God for His call and claim on their lives.

CHAPTER 3

Who Are the Called?

ESSENTIAL TRUTH

Every believer is called to *"walk worthy of the calling"* with which he or she was called.

> *I, therefore, the prisoner of the Lord, beseech you to walk worthy of the calling with which you were called, with all lowliness and gentleness, with longsuffering, bearing with one another in love, endeavoring to keep the unity of the Spirit in the bond of peace.*
>
> —EPHESIANS 4:1–3

> *"For the eyes of the LORD run to and fro throughout the whole earth, to show Himself strong on behalf of those whose heart is loyal to Him."*
>
> —2 CHRONICLES 16:9

Charles Beaty

"We Are Not Promised Tomorrow"

"Whom shall I send, and who will go for Us?" Then I said, "Here am I! Send me."

—ISAIAH 6:8

C harles and Christy Beaty heard God's call to them in 1994, and their answer was, "Here am I! Send me." One year later, the Beatys found themselves in northern Africa as career missionaries.

They had not grown up dreaming of becoming missionaries. Charles and Christy were focused on their insurance business, settling down in Kansas City, Kansas, and raising a family. Yet they responded to God's call, believing that people living with little or no access to the gospel needed to hear the message that Jesus Christ is Lord.

After serving for two years in North Africa, Charles and Christy received some devastating news. Charles, aged 30, had adenocarcinoma of the lung, a very serious form of lung cancer. Charles battled it for several years, but when he was 34, the doctors told him that he would be dead in just a few months.

Charles decided to spend the final months of his life mobilizing Christians to reach a lost and dying world for Jesus

Christ. His words challenge us to respond now to God's call: "Is the Lord calling you today to go—to go to the people who have no voice? My challenge to you is go, and don't wait, because we are not promised tomorrow."

Asked how he wanted to be remembered, Charles said, "I want them to think of the peoples of North Africa who will die and go into eternity hopeless without Christ. I want them to think, 'I'm going to go and live out my life for Jesus.'"

Charles Stuart Beaty died on October 2, 2001, but his life continues to remind us that we must make the most of every opportunity to share Jesus Christ with a lost world.

Quotes from Charles Beaty are used by permission of the International Mission Board of the Southern Baptist Convention.

ALL ARE CALLED

You may still be asking, "But just who are the called? Are they a special group of persons? What about my life? Am I called, too? How would I know? What would it sound like?"

Your heart may sincerely be saying, "Lord, I do love You! I do belong to You! I am Your servant, and I truly want to serve You. But Lord, am I really called to be on mission with You in my world? Lord, just who are the called?"

Unfortunately, our "Christian culture" has not always been thoroughly biblical. That is, as we have made a difference between clergy and laypeople, so we have made a difference between the specially called and the common believer. In reality, all believers are the called! The differences lie not in whether we are called or not, but in the nature of the assignment given by God. But every believer is one who is called by God, for Him to be free to accomplish His purposes in them and through them!

Let's look briefly at some Scripture passages that assure us that every believer is called. In Exodus 19, when God created a special nation through whom He would bring salvation to the whole world, He said:

> "'You have seen what I did to the Egyptians, and how I bore you on eagles' wings and brought you to Myself. Now therefore, if you will indeed obey My voice and keep My

*covenant, then you shall be a special treasure to Me above
all people; for all the earth is Mine. And you shall be to Me
a kingdom of priests and a holy nation.' These are the words
which you shall speak to the children of Israel."*

—Exodus 19:4–6

Did you notice that God said they
would be a "kingdom of priests"—not
a kingdom with a priesthood? Each and
every one of them would be priests unto
God. The Levites would be the ones
assigned to train and equip the entire

> *God said they would
> be a "kingdom of
> priests"—not a kingdom
> with a priesthood.*

nation to walk with God as priests unto God so He could fulfill
His purposes to save the nations of the world through them.
This same truth is stated in the New Testament.

> *You also, as living stones, are being built up a spiritual house,
> a holy priesthood, to offer up spiritual sacrifices acceptable to
> God through Jesus Christ. . . .*
>
> *But you are a chosen generation, a royal priesthood,
> a holy nation, His own special people, that you may pro-
> claim the praises of Him who called you out of darkness into
> His marvelous light; who once were not a people but are
> now the people of God, who had not obtained mercy but
> now have obtained mercy.*

—1 Peter 2:5, 9–10

Notice how Paul addressed the people of the church at Rome:

> *Through Him we have received grace and apostleship for obedience to the faith among all nations for His name, among whom you also are the called of Jesus Christ.*
>
> —ROMANS 1:5–6

For what does Paul say he received grace and apostleship? Yes, it was for obedience to the faith. There is little question that those who receive salvation from God have, at the same time, released themselves to the call of obedience that comes from faith. They go hand in hand. When you received Christ into your life, did you understand that, at that same moment, you were releasing your life to be used any way God would choose?

> *When you received Christ into your life, did you understand that, at that same moment, you were releasing your life to be used any way God would choose?*

Each believer is called of God and is to function before God and a watching world as a priest unto God. God, therefore, promised that He would enable every believer to function this way by the empowering presence of His Holy Spirit. God eternally planned that every believer would be spiritually equipped to both know and do the will of God, as He would reveal it to each one. In 1 Corinthians 2, we see this truth described vividly:

But God has revealed them to us through His Spirit. For the Spirit searches all things, yes, the deep things of God. For what man knows the things of a man except the spirit of the man which is in him? Even so no one knows the things of God except the Spirit of God. Now we have received, not the spirit of the world, but the Spirit who is from God, that we might know the things that have been freely given to us by God. These things we also speak, not in words which man's wisdom teaches but which the Holy Spirit teaches, comparing spiritual things with spiritual.

—1 CORINTHIANS 2:10–13

Did you notice what the Holy Spirit knows about the things of God and why God gave His children the gift of His Holy Spirit? The Holy Spirit has been given so that we can know what has been freely given to us by God. As you live out the call of God on your life, the heavenly Father will shape your life and provide all you need to follow Him. As He provides for your life, the Holy Spirit has been assigned to help you recognize and experience all the provision of God for your life.

There is no separation or distinction in the call of God between Christian leaders and other Christians. All Christians are called to a saving faith, and in this call, all must release their lives to God for His purposes.

While Dana and I served in Canada, we visited a wonderful church in Calgary, Alberta. In fact, it was the largest Christian church in western Canada. At the beginning of each year, the pastor gave an address (like a State of the Union address). He made an incredible statement related to the many ministries of the church: he said that most all of the church's successful ministries were created from suggestions and heartfelt convictions of the members of the congregation rather than being devised by the staff. He then encouraged the congregation that if persons in the church had burdens on their hearts for new ministries, they should bring those burdens to the staff so they could make the necessary adjustments to help meet their requests. Here was the pastor of a church with thousands of people attending each weekend who recognized the vital role each member had in the ministry. No wonder this church was making a significant impact in the city and province as they ministered to special-needs families, low-income homes, the homeless, senior adults, and so on.

When we consider the following words by Paul in 1 Corinthians 1, we can easily identify the qualifications for being *called of God*.

> *For you see your calling, brethren, that not many wise according to the flesh, not many mighty, not many noble, are called. But God has chosen the foolish things of the world to put to shame the wise, and God has chosen the weak things*

*of the world to put to shame the things which are mighty;
and the base things of the world and the things which are
despised God has chosen, and the things which are not, to
bring to nothing the things that are, that no flesh should glory
in His presence. But of Him you are in Christ Jesus, who
became for us wisdom from God—and righteousness and
sanctification and redemption—that, as it is written, "He
who glories, let him glory in the LORD."*

—1 CORINTHIANS 1:26–31

Why does God choose or call the foolish, weak, base, and despised things to use as His instruments?

Many times we have seen people in various stages of life who say that they are just ordinary people with no special gifts or abilities. They usually say, "I don't know what God could use me to do." Have you ever excluded yourself from service to God because you did not feel qualified? Based on this passage, do you think that God could and does desire to use your life in His kingdom? Yes, when God saved you, He had a plan to use your life in redeeming a lost world! Too many times, we limit what God might want to do in us because of self. God chooses to use the weak things in this world to reveal Himself to a watching world. Don't let your opinion of yourself limit what God might want to do through you. Release your life to God and let Him do more than you could ask or imagine through your life that will show a watching world His power—bringing glory to Him.

I was asked to teach a spiritual leadership class at a church I was attending in the Atlanta area. The class was small, but some really outstanding people were attending. I looked at the group and noticed several influential and successful people were in the class. As I prepared each week, I tried to make sure to address some of the issues these men—owners of their own businesses and leaders in the church—would face.

One man attending the group drove a truck for a package delivery company. He had worked for this company for about 20 years and always had some kind of encouraging word about the people he met along the route. I watched Ron grow each week and listened to him share how he was taking the truths of the study and applying them to his week. Over the period I was teaching the class, we became good friends, and the friendship has grown over the years. I watched Ron as he released his life to God and God began to use him in the workplace. I have watched as fellow co-workers, bosses, family members, and customers have sought out Ron in times of distress. God has used him to help families of troubled teens, to encourage people with terminal illness, and to give marriage counsel to men in great need. To this day, if someone calls me in deep spiritual need in the Atlanta area, I do not give them a pastor's number, I put them in contact with Ron. When I think back to the beginnings of that spiritual leadership class, I laugh when I think how wrong

I was about whom God was going to use among those men. God chose to use the one I least expected, and when you hear Ron share, it is clear that God always receives the glory.

COMPLETENESS OF GOD'S CALL

When God calls someone, He does it completely. Have you noticed the extensiveness and completeness of God's call and God's equipping of all people—sons, daughters, young men and women, middle-aged adults, and old men and women? This includes you too!

> *Their abilities or skills were not as important as their relationship with God.*

Another interesting and encouraging realization is that throughout the Bible, most of the people God called and worked through mightily were what we today would call everyday believers. They were ordinary people called and enabled by God to work with Him in their world. Their abilities or skills were not as important as their relationship with God. Their heart relationship of love and trust in God always determined how much God was able to do through them.

> *He also chose David His servant,*
> *And took him from the sheepfolds;*
> *From following the ewes that had young He brought him,*
> *To shepherd Jacob His people,*
> *And Israel His inheritance.*

So he shepherded them according to the integrity of his heart,
And guided them by the skillfulness of his hands.

—PSALM 78:70–72

David was a shepherd, and God chose him for a very special assignment: God would guide His people through him.

According to Scripture, Amos said he was not a prophet or son of a prophet—just a sheep breeder:

"I was no prophet,
Nor was I a son of a prophet,
But I was a sheepbreeder
And a tender of sycamore fruit.
Then the LORD took me as I followed the flock,
And the LORD said to me,
'Go, prophesy to My people Israel.' "

—AMOS 7:14–15

Peter was a fisherman. He and all the other disciples were what we would call just ordinary people—until God assigned them roles in His kingdom where He would work through them mightily to accomplish His purposes. This has continued to be God's way to this very day. I (Henry) watched God do this for more than 30 years as I served as a pastor among God's people.

Let's take a look at some ordinary people in the Scriptures whom God called and used in extravagant ways.

In Joshua 2:1, the Bible describes Rahab as a harlot. However, if we follow Rahab's life, we see that God used her life to accomplish His purposes for Israel. Rahab and her whole family were saved when God gave the city of Jericho to Israel. She was an ordinary person who recognized God's activity in His people (Joshua 2:9–11), and God used her life in extraordinary ways. Notice in Matthew 1:5 in the genealogy of Jesus that Rahab is listed as the mother of Boaz. She is also described in Hebrews 11:31 and James 2:25 as a woman of faith and of works.

Luke, described as a physician in Colossians 4:14, accompanied the Apostle Paul in his missionary tour of Asia and Macedonia (see Acts 16:10–13, when Luke joined Paul, and Acts 20:5–6), to Jerusalem (Acts 21:1–18), and to Rome (Acts 27 28; 2 Timothy 4:11; Philemon 24). God called a doctor, made him a disciple, and sent him into service. When you read about all that happened to Paul, can you see why God would place a doctor with him on his travels? Here is Paul's record of all that had happened to him during the missionary journeys:

From the Jews five times I received forty stripes minus one. Three times I was beaten with rods; once I was stoned; three times I was shipwrecked; a night and a day I have been in the deep; in journeys often, in perils of waters, in perils of robbers, in perils of my own countrymen, in perils of the Gentiles, in perils in the city, in perils in the wilderness, in perils in the sea, in perils among false brethren; in weariness

*and toil, in sleeplessness often, in hunger and thirst, in
fastings often, in cold and nakedness.*

—2 CORINTHIANS 11:24–27

God worked in the life of Luke, preparing him long beforehand
to fulfill the call upon his life to be a companion to Paul. Not
only did God use Luke to walk with
Paul as he shared the gospel to the
Gentiles, but God had other plans
for this servant: Luke was chosen to
record the life and ministry of Jesus as
well as the history of the early church
in the Gospel of Luke and the Book
of Acts. When we consider all of
the writings in the New Testament,
we see that Luke wrote more than
any other single author. This ordinary physician was used in
extraordinary ways by God.

> *The key is not our
> talents, but the cultivat-
> ing of our hearts, so when
> God does work through
> us, we offer the praise
> to Him and let others
> know it was God who
> accomplished the work.*

How ordinary is your life compared with God's special
assignment for you? He chooses the ordinary and the ones the
world would not choose, so that when He has completed His
work, He alone will receive the glory. The key is not our talents, but the cultivating of our hearts, so when God does work
through us, we offer the praise to Him and let others know it was
God who accomplished the work.

No believer should let fear of failure prevent him or her from responding fully to the call of God. Everything needed for life and godliness has been provided and is immediately at work in every life that obeys God's call.

> *Grace and peace be multiplied to you in the knowledge of God and of Jesus our Lord, as His divine power has given to us all things that pertain to life and godliness, through the knowledge of Him who called us by glory and virtue, by which have been given to us exceedingly great and precious promises, that through these you may be partakers of the divine nature, having escaped the corruption that is in the world through lust.*
>
> —2 Peter 1:2–4

Spend some time in prayer right now, and ask God if your fear of failure has limited His working in and through your life.

Jesus Equips the Called

You may be thinking that you are not equipped to live out the call of God. Remember, in John 17, Jesus revealed to us that the Father gives our lives to Jesus for Him to develop and teach us. For what purpose? To make us useful vessels that His Father can use to save a lost and dying world. In His significant prayer, Jesus said to the Father:

> "I have glorified You on the earth. I have finished the work which You have given Me to do.... I have manifested Your name to the men whom You have given Me out of the world. They were Yours, You gave them to Me, and they have kept Your word. Now they have known that all things which You have given Me are from You. For I have given to them the words which You have given Me; and they have received them, and have known surely that I came forth from You; and they have believed that You sent Me.... And the glory which You gave Me I have given them, that they may be one just as We are one: I in them, and You in Me; that they may be made perfect in one, and that the world may know that You have sent Me, and have loved them as You have loved Me."
>
> —JOHN 17:4, 6–8, 22–23

When Jesus called the first disciples, He assured them of His responsibility for their lives: *"Then Jesus said to them, 'Follow Me, and I will make you become fishers of men'"* (Mark 1:17).

Whose responsibility was it for the disciples to become fishers of men? Jesus would be the One who, under the instruction of the Father, would teach the disciples of the kingdom of God, for which they would, in turn, give their lives and become fishers of men. The disciples were simply responsible to stay with Jesus and learn and practice what He taught.

> *"This is the will of the Father who sent Me, that of all He has given Me I should lose nothing, but should raise it up at the last day."*
>
> —JOHN 6:39

All of the Gospels record how Jesus taught, trained, guided, encouraged, empowered, and fully equipped His disciples for all that the Father had in mind to do through them. Have you ever considered how Jesus has been equipping you for all that the heavenly Father has in mind for your life?

FROM NORMAN: A CRIMINAL JUSTICE DEGREE

While I was in college, I pursued a degree in criminal justice and history because I planned to go to law school and become an attorney. After earning my college degree, I was on my way from Texas to Vancouver, British Columbia, with the intent to pursue my planned career when God encountered me and put on my heart that I was to go to seminary. I turned around and went back to Texas to enroll in school. As I completed my master's degree work, God led me into the PhD program. During this same time, He also called me to pastor my first church. Looking back on my life, I can see how God was preparing me for ministry, even with a degree in criminal justice. In my first church, I used my knowledge of criminal justice often as I counseled broken families and helped give direction to church members who came from a variety of backgrounds. Now, years later, I see how God continues to shape my life in a variety of ways for His kingdom purposes. God is faithful to train, guide, encourage, and empower those who are called and accountable! While I was pursuing a career plan in college, God was preparing and equipping me for His purposes.

> *Our living Lord has accepted your life from the Father and is at work in you, that you may become all God wants you to be.*

John 17 reveals just how thoroughly Jesus prepared the disciples for their mission in their world. You and I are included in that very prayer in John 17. As Jesus said, *"I do not pray for these alone, but also for those who will believe in Me through their word"* (John 17:20). So you need not be concerned that you are not prepared to be of use to God.

Our living Lord has accepted your life from the Father and is at work in you, that you may become all God wants you to be.

ORDINARY PEOPLE—IMPORTANT TO GOD

Each one of us is important to God! We are ordinary people who love God with all our hearts and who know that the call to salvation is also a call to be laborers together with God in our world. As we respond to the call of God and yield to Him, He powerfully accomplishes His purpose to save a lost world through our lives. God seeks out those who are willing to stand before Him on behalf of the land:

> *"So I sought for a man among them who would make a wall, and stand in the gap before Me on behalf of the land, that I should not destroy it; but I found no one. Therefore I have poured out My indignation on them; I have consumed them with the fire of My wrath; and I have recompensed their deeds on their own heads," says the Lord GOD.*
>
> —EZEKIEL 22:30–31

If He does not find a person to *"stand in the gap,"* the land and the people are destroyed. But when He does find someone who will do the job, He is able to save multitudes of people.

When Jonah finally obeyed God's assignment to take His message to the people of the great city of Nineveh, the king and all the people responded with immediate and thorough repentance, and the entire city was saved. This was the intent of God's heart, and it waited on the obedience of an ordinary child of God.

We may not understand why God chooses to use individuals and often waits on their response before He acts, *but that He chooses to work through His people is very clear.* If we have been unwilling to be the ones whom God could use as His instruments, then we must ask ourselves, "What could have been if only I had responded immediately to God's invitation to join Him in His heart for the lost?" We can get caught up in our own worlds and not recognize that the lives of people hang in the balance as God waits on our response to Him.

> And Mordecai told them to answer Esther: "Do not think in your heart that you will escape in the king's palace any more than all the other Jews. For if you remain completely silent at this time, relief and deliverance will arise for the Jews from another place, but you and your father's house will perish. Yet who knows whether you have come to the kingdom for such a time as this?"
>
> —ESTHER 4:13–14

Esther was a very ordinary woman. But she had *"come to the kingdom for such a time as this."* Her response was vital to the heart of God for His people. Their lives and destiny hung in the balance and, at that very time, in the hands of Esther. She literally risked her life as God worked through her to save His people. And we know of her life and deeds to this very day.

Many other women were just as vital. For example, Hannah brought forth the great prophet, priest, and judge, Samuel. Deborah saved God's people from their enemies (Judges 4–5). Elizabeth and Mary were available to God for bringing John the Baptist and Jesus into the world. And Mary Magdalene was greatly used of God, one day at a time, to minister to Jesus and His disciples and was, therefore, greatly honored of God.

Are you of a heart to respond to the Lord the way Isaiah did?

Also I heard the voice of the Lord, saying:
"Whom shall I send,
And who will go for Us?"
Then I said, "Here am I! Send me."
—Isaiah 6:8

Often people look at Isaiah's response and feel that it is only for being sent to a great task. We can be looking for the booming voice of God calling out to see who will go forth to a worthwhile and visible ministry. However, God is looking over your home, church, community, city, and beyond when He asks, *"Whom shall I send?"* *"Whom shall I send* into the schools or to the soccer and football fields?" *"Whom shall I send* into the community cen-ter, the hospitals, and the business place?" If we are not careful, we can miss the activity of God and His invitation for us to join Him while we wait for a "big" assignment. How many people are missing out on hearing the gospel and how many children or young people make do without discipleship because no one responds to God's call to teach a Sunday School class or share their faith at work?

We need to be reminded of another Scripture:

"For the eyes of the LORD run to and fro throughout the whole earth, to show Himself strong on behalf of those whose heart is loyal to Him."

—2 CHRONICLES 16:9

What is God looking over the earth to do, according to this passage? Does it surprise you that God is looking for someone to use and work in to display His strength to a watching world? What do you think the Lord sees when He looks at your life? This verse should serve as an encouragement to every Christian. He does not need our strengths, our talents, or our plans; He simply wants our willing, obedient hearts. If we make our lives available to Him, He will, in turn, strengthen, empower, and equip us (show Himself strong in us) to accomplish His will so that the watching world will see His love.

Could God describe your heart as being loyal to Him? Do your actions reveal a heart that is loyal to Him?

FROM HENRY: BEING PREPARED AND AVAILABLE

Gerry and Brenda Wortman had not been married long. Gerry had just become a Christian. As they studied the Bible, seeking to be faithful, they realized that they must be as prepared and as available to God as possible. This is what the Scriptures revealed to them. They came to attend the theological college we had established in our church to gain some basic knowledge of God and His Word. As they studied, God saw their hearts and, through unusual circumstances, led them to a First Nations reservation in Canada to teach the Bible. By the time they completed their three years of study, God had given them hearts for the native peoples and special skills to enable them to minister to them.

God reached many people through Gerry and Brenda. Later they were called to pastor a mission for First Nations people and, then, to a position directing First Nations ministries for all of Canada. Currently, Gerry is a pastor of a church in Saskatchewan, and, of course, the church has several ministries to First Nations peoples. He and Brenda have also adopted four First Nations children!

Two lives were called to salvation, and these two realized that the call to salvation was a call to be fully available for God's purpose to win a lost world, wherever He would choose to send them. What a difference they have made! And that sense of purpose has captured their lives.

PRAYER & APPLICATION

You can never fully estimate the value of your life to God. To God, eternity is always at stake! Your obedience releases the fullness of God in accomplishing His purpose to redeem a lost world and even to inaugurate eternity in His fullness of time.

Spend time in prayer, asking God to reveal to you His will for using you. Do you sense that God is looking over your life and asking you to go with Him to touch your world? Do you know of some areas in which He has been asking you to serve, but you have not responded? How is He sending you, as a child of God, to be involved in His work?

Taking a Spiritual Inventory

Now is an appropriate time to take a spiritual inventory! In light of all the Scriptures you have studied, with the Holy Spirit as your teacher, the inventory will help you evaluate your relationship with God.

Such an inventory is necessary for every sincere believer! Too often Christians want to have, for example, the *"faith of Abraham."* But they do not realize that it took God about 40 years to develop Abraham's character to the point where he would immediately respond to God's command to offer his only son, Isaac, as a sacrifice to God. During those years of development, God often reviewed His covenant with Abraham found in Genesis 12:1–3.

God also brought Moses constantly before Him to remind him of his walk with God. He did this with David as well, and in Psalm 51, we see the major changes David had to make to *"restore* to [him] the joy of [God's] salvation" (v. 12). Jesus had to take His disciples aside constantly to explain how their continuing lack of faith was affecting their relationship with Him.

God must take each of us aside regularly, remind us of His call in our lives, bring to our remembrance all He has said to us (see John 14:26), and help us see how we are responding to His shaping and guiding of our lives.

A spiritual inventory must be done in the presence of God! He alone has lordship in our lives. To God alone are we accountable. Therefore, it is before Him and in His presence that we must stand for a spiritual evaluation—done

> *To God alone are we accountable. Therefore, it is before Him and in His presence that we must stand for a spiritual evaluation—done by God Himself.*

by God Himself. You may sense that He is saying, "Well done, good and faithful servant. You have been faithful in a little, I can now give you more!" (see Matthew 25:21, 23). Or you may sense God is grieved and is exclaiming, "Why do you keep calling Me 'Lord! Lord!' yet never do anything that I say?" (see Luke 6:46).

> *But we all, with unveiled face, beholding as in a mirror the glory of the Lord, are being transformed into the same image from glory to glory, just as by the Spirit of the Lord.*
>
> —2 Corinthians 3:18

Paul assured believers that they could stand face-to-face with God, with "no veil" between them and God. But he said that when they stood face-to-face with God, they would be *"transformed into the same image from glory to glory"* (2 Corinthians 3:18). When a believer is face-to-face with God, an automatic "inventory" is taken by God to check out Christlikeness! When we stand before God, we become very aware of our own lives. Do you remember Peter's response when he encountered Jesus in his fishing boat and acknowledged Him as Lord? *"Depart from me, for I am a sinful man, O Lord!"* (Luke 5:8). Isaiah had a similar response when he met God in the Temple as he stated, *"Woe is me, for I am undone! Because I am a man of unclean lips, and I dwell in the midst of a people of unclean lips; for my eyes have seen the King, the* LORD *of hosts"* (Isaiah 6:5). Both of these men ultimately were used of God, but when they met the Lord, they saw themselves as God saw them, and they submitted their lives to God.

This standing before God comes when we, with transparent honesty, present ourselves for the *"washing of water by the word"* (Ephesians 5:26–27). The regular reading and study of God's Word is a must for every believer.

Prayer also brings us into God's presence, where God changes our ways into His ways, and we cry out as Jesus did, *"Not my will, but thine, be done"* (Luke 22:42 KJV).

In summary, here are the important ingredients of a spiritual inventory:

1. Do it before God.
2. Do it with prayer and His Word as your plumb line, or standard.
3. Do it with transparent honesty.
4. Do it thoroughly.
5. Ask the right questions:
   - Am I a believer?
   - Do I therefore know that I am called by God?
   - Does this include being on mission with God?
   - Does my life give constant evidence that I have released my life fully to Him?

MY SPIRITUAL INVENTORY

Date: _____

As you consider your life, list key events in which God has
clearly directed you.

_____

_____

_____

_____

_____

_____

_____

_____

Now, as you look back over the last year, can you see areas in
which God has been working in your life?

_____

_____

_____

_____

_____

_____

_____

_____

As you reflect on God's activity in your life, list adjustments you have made in order to join Him in His activity.

_____

_____

_____

_____

_____

Should the Holy Spirit remind you of some "unfinished" business (something you have known that God wanted you to do, but you never adjusted your life to obey), write it below and make a commitment to quickly adjust your life so that you can obey in this area.

_____

_____

_____

_____

_____

Take time to ask the Lord to show you what He thinks of your life and of your obedience to Him. What is His response? Be ready to make adjustments in your life in order to respond to His perspective of your life.

_____

_____

Arthur and Marion Clark

An Ordinary Couple Who Affected Eternity

Arthur served in the business world as an accountant all his life. He was a faithful deacon in our church, serving wherever he was asked. Marion was committed to prayer and to missions. Under the preaching of God's Word, they both felt God had something more for their lives. They felt led to be available to God and to their church by being a lay pastor and wife team in an attempted church plant in the Russian community just north of our city. The church saw their lives and affirmed their sense of call—ordinary people, but now called of God to serve in church planting.

They served in this Russian community for six years, leading many children, some youth, and several adults to the Lord. However, this community was a very closed community, and not one person came for baptism or to join the new work. Arthur and Marion were often disheartened. This was their first experience in church planting. The entire church and I, as their pastor, saw their devotion to the Lord and affirmed them. Arthur even taught accounting at our theological college. Arthur was diagnosed with cancer and eventually died. But the influence of their lives affected their daughter and her husband, who then pastored faithfully for many years. Now Arthur and Marion's grandson is pastoring in Arkansas and is a highly respected pastor.

An ordinary couple, clearly sensing God's call and responding with a sacred accountability to that call, affected eternity for many who would not otherwise have known the Savior and, in turn, affected their own family to at least two generations. Although they may not have seen all the visible fruit in the church plant where they served, fruit was abundant indeed. Their faithfulness was an inspiration to countless church members who were, in turn, called to ministry in various ways. Arthur's willingness to serve in the college touched the lives of many, and generations of Arthur and Marion's own family have been impacted by the spiritual heritage they created. Their service will be rewarded in heaven.

Chapter 4

How Am I Called?

Essential Truth

God rarely does the same thing twice, for He desires that every person believe Him and have faith in Him—not in a method! Throughout the Bible and in history, through the testimonies of those God has used mightily, every person's call has been deliberately unique.

> "If anyone serves Me, let him follow Me; and where I am, there My servant will be also. If anyone serves Me, him My Father will honor."
>
> —John 12:26

Harold Ray Watson
A New Way to Be Salt

In 1965 Harold Watson, his wife, Joyce, and their three small boys arrived in Mlang, Cotabato, a small town in the center of Mindanao, the Philippines. Harold and his family had been appointed as missionaries; they were to be "agriculture evangelists" on the second-largest island in the Philippines.

Harold had never heard of agricultural evangelism while growing up on a farm in rural Mississippi. He liked farming and wondered if someday he might be able to have his own farm. While serving in the air force on the island of Okinawa during the Korean War, Harold believed that God was calling him to be a missionary. Harold began to think that there might be a new way to share the gospel of Jesus Christ in foreign lands through his love of farming.

Upon arriving in the Philippines, Harold observed that many of the Filipinos were impoverished and malnourished. Most of the steep land was not suited for traditional farming, so the people had little to eat and no way to make even a meager income. Harold decided to set up a demonstration farm on 50 acres of land and develop a method of farming that would help the Filipinos be able to feed themselves.

The 50 acres of land became known as the Mindanao Baptist Rural Life Center. Harold gradually developed a farming method called sloping agricultural land technology (SALT) that enables local farmers to produce food on badly eroded hillsides. Training programs at the center introduce people to the new farming method and to Jesus Christ. The students return to their villages with the ability to provide physical and spiritual food for their families.

SALT has been adopted by a variety of countries (including Indonesia, Sri Lanka, Burma, and many other Asian countries) and relief organizations to battle hunger. Some 18,000 people visit the center every year to learn SALT.

Jesus said to His disciples, *"You are the salt of the earth"* (Matthew 5:13). God showed Harold Watson a new way to be salt in a lost world.

You Must Clearly Know Him

Before a person can fully understand the question, "How am I called?" he or she must clearly and unmistakably know God. Jesus defined eternal life this way: *"And this is eternal life, that they may know You, the only true God, and Jesus Christ whom You have sent"* (John 17:3). *To know* Jesus Christ is to *"perceive, recognize, become acquainted with, and understand"* Him and His ways (see John 17:3 AMP).

So crucial was this thorough knowledge of Jesus Christ to the purposes of God that the Father taught the disciples through Jesus how to have this relationship. It was almost three years into Jesus's ministry before Jesus finally asked them, *"Who do you say that I am?"* (Matthew 16:15). When Peter responded that Jesus was *"the Christ, the Son of the Living God,"* Jesus assured him that he was right: *"Flesh and blood has not revealed this to you, but My Father who is in heaven."* Only then, with the disciples fully committed to who He was, was He able for the first time to introduce them to His cross and His coming death (see Matthew 16:16–17, 21).

Jesus, one form of the Triune God, is described many different ways in the Scriptures. Take a moment to read the following list and meditate on these names of God. (These are only a few of His names.)

- Advocate *(1 John 2:1)*
- Almighty *(Revelation 1:8)*

- Alpha and Omega *(Revelation 1:8)*
- Author and Finisher/Perfecter of our faith *(Hebrews 12:2)*
- Bread of life *(John 6:48)*
- Captain of salvation *(Hebrews 2:10)*
- Christ the power of God *(1 Corinthians 1:24)*
- Christ the wisdom of God *(1 Corinthians 1:24)*
- Counselor *(Isaiah 9:6)*
- Deliverer *(Romans 11:26)*
- Door *(John 10:7)*
- Eternal life *(1 John 5:20; John 10:28)*
- Faithful and True *(Revelation 19:11)*
- Friend of sinners *(Matthew 11:19)*
- Gift of God *(John 4:10)*
- Savior *(Isaiah 45:15; John 4:42)*
- Great Shepherd of the sheep *(Hebrews 13:20)*
- Judge *(Acts 10:42)*
- Light of the world *(John 8:12)*
- Lord God Almighty *(Revelation 15:3)*
- The Lord, your Redeemer *(Isaiah 43:14)*

Can you identify with any of these names of God? For example, you have personally come to know Jesus as your Savior (Isaiah 45:15; John 4:42) and the giver of eternal life (1 John 5:20; John 10:28). Or you might be thinking of a time when He was your Counselor (Isaiah 9:6) or your Deliverer

(Romans 11:26). Has He ever been your Advocate (1 John 2:1)? Or, as you consider all of the ways He has provided for you, would you describe Him as the Bread of life (John 6:48)?

If you are struggling to describe your relationship with Jesus based on these names of God, take time to pray and ask the Lord to reveal Himself more clearly to you.

Many times in our ministry, God has revealed to us that persons *can* be active in a church or involved in Christian activities without truly knowing Him. We must each carefully examine our relationship with Jesus Christ and know that we *know* Him before we can answer the question, "How am I called?"

Further, we must be sure that *He knows us*. At the close of Jesus' Sermon on the Mount, He makes a very powerful statement about salvation:

> *"Not everyone who says to Me, 'Lord, Lord,' shall enter the kingdom of heaven, but he who does the will of My Father in heaven. Many will say to Me in that day, 'Lord, Lord, have we not prophesied in Your name, cast out demons in Your name, and done many wonders in Your name?' And then I will declare to them, 'I never knew you; depart from Me, you who practice lawlessness!'"*
>
> —MATTHEW 7:21–23

Our relationship is not based on our activities or our claims that we know Him. Jesus did not deny the wonders the people had done; He simply said He did not know them. They had never entered into a personal intimate fellowship with Him. He was not the Lord of their lives, regardless of their claims or activities. This is a serious question every person needs to settle with God. Does He know me? What is the evidence that I am in a vital intimate fellowship with the Lord?

Without this God-given heart understanding of who Jesus is, all else is useless. It is a vital part of the Father's plan. But it is not merely head knowledge. It must move down and take residence in the heart! The heart determines every other response to God (Mark 7:14–23; Proverbs 4:23). On our response rests the eternal purpose of God being worked out through us.

PRAYER & APPLICATION

Every believer must have a thorough, God-given, real, and personal relationship with Jesus Christ. The entire Christian life depends on it!

How long has it been since you took time to share your testimony with someone? The longer we know Christ, the more we should be able to share our life-changing relationship with others. Take time to write out your testimony in your spiritual journal, and describe how you have been growing in your understanding and fellowship with Christ from the time of your salvation.

Awareness of God's Call

We have already indicated that the initial call is a call to salvation, a call to become a child of God and servant of Jesus Christ. It is an eternal decision and an eternal relationship. But from the moment you are born again, how are you called by God and placed on mission with Him?

When Jesus is Lord, His servant always responds, "Yes, Lord!"

For a Christian to seriously ask the question, "How am I called?" the Christian must bring with this question a personal commitment both to respond and to be accountable to God in the calling. When the Christian senses that God is guiding him or her to a clear, simple answer to this question, that person will also be deeply, even painfully, aware that having the knowledge of His will immediately brings with it a solemn sense of accountability.

From the moment when you sense God is calling you, you can never be the same again! You will have to make a conscious decision to say, "Yes, Lord!" Be aware that you may tend to say no, but you cannot say, "No, Lord!" For if you say no, at that moment, He is no longer Lord of your life. When Jesus is Lord, His servant always responds, "Yes, Lord!"

Many forget that when a person first becomes a Christian, that person is a "baby" Christian who must then grow and learn to use the newly given "spiritual senses." That newborn Christian needs to learn to function with his or her newly provided spiritual family, the local church. This takes time and experience, just as it does in the physical birth and growth experience.

The context for this growth, as designed and provided by God, is the local church. God does not bring a person into His kingdom without adequate provision for protection, learning, feeding, and being loved. In the local church, we learn about our new lives in Christ and are given the opportunities to learn to walk, talk, share, and gain experiences.

New believers must first receive the *"milk of the word"* (1 Peter 2:2). As they grow, they are carefully taken from milk to meat (Hebrews 5:12–14). Someone on "meat" would be described as a teacher of the Word, or someone who is continually moving beyond the beginning truths of the faith, who puts into practice and applies the truths of God consistently (Hebrews 5:12–14; 1 Corinthians 3:1–3).

Often we may think we are mature in the faith simply because we have been Christians for many years. However, the Bible describes maturity by how we learn and understand the Word of God, implement the truths of God into our lives, and allow God to use us to teach others to grow in the faith.

It is important to note that the passage in Hebrews was an address to all the people and not simply the leaders. Each person was expected to grow and, in turn, teach others who were young in the faith. They should become teachers of the Word and, by skillful use of the Word, move from milk to meat. The church must help each believer to grow this way, to become mature and able to be of greater and greater use to God. Paul continually speaks of becoming "mature."

> Not that I have already attained, or am already perfected; but I press on, that I may lay hold of that for which Christ Jesus has also laid hold of me. Brethren, I do not count myself to have apprehended; but one thing I do, forgetting those things which are behind and reaching forward to those things which are ahead, I press toward the goal for the prize of the upward call of God in Christ Jesus. Therefore let us, as many as are mature, have this mind; and if in anything you think otherwise, God will reveal even this to you.
>
> —PHILIPPIANS 3:12–15

But all this takes time! It also takes obedience to Christ, who commanded believers not only to *"make disciples"* and baptize them, but also to teach them to observe all things He had commanded them (Matthew 28:19–20). This task is spiritually demanding but was faithfully practiced by early believers in Jerusalem, as seen in Acts 2:41–47. This is a simple and clear picture of a spiritual family, the local church, taking care of newborn believers. As you read the rest of the Book of Acts, you see how those believers soon were on mission with God all over their world. God really did accomplish His eternal purpose to redeem the lost through them.

Let's take a moment to read this passage from Acts 2. As you read, take notice of the things the early church did to help their members mature in Christ.

> *Then those who gladly received his word were baptized; and that day about three thousand souls were added to them.*
>
> *And they continued steadfastly in the apostles' doctrine and fellowship, in the breaking of bread, and in prayers. Then fear came upon every soul, and many wonders and signs were done through the apostles. Now all who believed were together, and had all things in common, and sold their possessions and goods, and divided them among all, as anyone had need. So continuing daily with one accord in the temple, and breaking bread from house to house, they ate their food with gladness and simplicity of heart, praising God and having favor with all the people. And the Lord added to the church daily those who were being saved.*
>
> —Acts 2:41–47

As we read this passage, we notice several things that are key to maturing in Christ:

✓ They gladly received the Word.
✓ They were baptized.
✓ They kept growing and developing their spiritual senses as they "*continued steadfastly*" in the apostles' doctrine, fellowship, breaking of bread (not just the Lord's Supper, but sharing meals together), and praying together.

✓ God's power was clearly seen as *"many wonders and signs were done through the apostles."*

✓ They were on the same page, spiritually—*"all who believed were together, and had all things in common."*

✓ They not only met each other's spiritual needs, but they met physical needs as well—*"sold their possessions and goods, and divided them among all, as anyone had need."*

✓ They were unified—so much so that they worshipped in *"one accord,"* shared meals with each other *"from house to house,"* did it with *"gladness and simplicity of heart,"* and praised God together (with unity).

The results are clearly seen in the final verse of the passage: *"having favor with all the people. And the Lord added to the church daily those who were being saved."* The natural progression is that as we study the Scriptures together, we will grow in our fellowship with each other. As our hearts grow tender towards God, we will grow tenderhearted towards others. As this discipleship was lived out in the early church, it could not go unnoticed in the community. The early church was radically different from anything else in the Roman world. In a day when people did not look out for one another and so many were isolated, people who encountered the early church saw something different.

God gave us a clear picture of incredible fellowship and unprecedented spiritual growth among His people. His desire is for every church to experience this same unity, fellowship, growth, and demonstration of His supernatural power in our day.

Is your church helping the members grow into maturity? As you consider how God used and called those in the early church, picture where your life fits into God's plan for your church. God's desire is that once you have entered into a relationship with Him, you grow into maturity in the Christian life and, in turn, be used to help others grow in their faith.

Below is a brief summary of the things new believers must be taught early in their Christian lives:

- To receive spiritual food regularly
- To develop their newly given "spiritual senses" (more about this in the next section)
- To develop a great sensitivity toward sin
- To learn the strategies of Satan (as Jesus did)
- To learn to resist Satan and sin with their whole beings
- To know (often the hard way) the consequences of sin and the crucial role of the church in restoring persons affected by sin
- To know the nature of a life of holiness, so they will always be available to God
- To know their places in the body (local church) and how their lives are used by God to edify and help others grow in the body of Christ

- To find out, as the disciples did, the nature of the
  kingdom of heaven and how God functions in their
  world, especially through prayer
- To know how to effectively share their faith and
  present the gospel to others

Having grown up in Christ, they will be gradually taken on
mission with God. As they are faithful in little things, God
will give them more and more significant opportunities to be on
mission with Him. In this process, they will learn to wait on
the Lord—to be still. In this being still and waiting, they will
learn some key secrets:

- How to yield their lives completely to God's working
  through them
- How to appropriate all that God has provided by His
  grace and by His presence within them

This will especially include Christ living out His life in them
and the complete sufficiency of the presence and power of the
Holy Spirit.

An awareness of God's call involves all this and much more.

SPIRITUAL SENSES DEVELOPED

As you grow, you will also develop "spiritual senses." First,
remember that when you are born again as a child of God, you

are given spiritual senses so you can hear and see and understand all the ways and activities of God.

> *And the disciples came and said to Him, "Why do You speak to them in parables?"*
>
> *He answered and said to them, "Because it has been given to you to know the mysteries of the kingdom of heaven, but to them it has not been given. For whoever has, to him more will be given, and he will have abundance; but whoever does not have, even what he has will be taken away from him. Therefore I speak to them in parables, because seeing they do not see, and hearing they do not hear, nor do they understand."*
>
> —MATTHEW 13:10–13

To whom did Jesus give the ability to understand the ways and thinking of His kingdom? That ability was given to the ones whom God had called, who once called, chose to follow Christ—the disciples. But not all persons are able to understand such things:

> *"And in them the prophecy of Isaiah is fulfilled, which says:*
> *'Hearing you will hear and shall not understand,*
> *And seeing you will see and not perceive;*
> *For the hearts of this people have grown dull.*
> *Their ears are hard of hearing,*
> *And their eyes they have closed,*

Lest they should see with their eyes and hear with their ears,
Lest they should understand with their hearts and turn,
So that I should heal them.'"

—Matthew 13:14–15

Did you notice the reason these people were unable to see, hear, and receive healing from God? It was because their hearts had grown dull, their ears were hard of hearing, and they chose to close their eyes. Your heart plays a vital role in hearing and following God's call on your life.

Jesus clearly indicated to His disciples that since they had been "called by God," they were different. For example, Jesus told them, *"It has been given to you to know the mysteries of the kingdom of heaven, but to them* [others around them] *it has not been given"* (Matthew 13:11). This was followed by this astounding announcement: *"But blessed are your eyes for they see, and your ears for they hear"* (Matthew 13:16). Every believer must develop the use of these special spiritual senses. It is by the use of them that one grows.

For everyone who partakes only of milk is unskilled in the word of righteousness, for he is a babe. But solid food belongs to those who are of full age, that is, those who by reason of use have their senses exercised to discern both good and evil.

—Hebrews 5:13–14

A newborn child is fully equipped with senses to function in the physical world. By the constant use of them, a child grows to maturity. I had to assist each of my children to use their eyes to see, their ears to hear, and their noses to smell. At each stage of their growth, they had new things to learn. I knew that if they grew normally, they could read and eventually attain to a PhD, if God called them to that task. Each of my children has gone on to receive seminary training and all are serving the Lord. But the day-by-day growth when they were younger was essential to what they would become.

I remember vividly some "senses training" my father did when we were staying in a cabin in Northern British Columbia. During the daylight hours, he took my two brothers and me deep into the forest and taught us to listen. We closed our eyes and listened for different sounds. We heard the chirping of a bird and the movement of it flying. We identified the noises of rustling leaves and found a little squirrel. We heard the wind blowing through the large trees. My father wanted us to hear these sounds during the day, so when we heard them at night, we wouldn't be frightened. We had the most wonderful time on our trip, and we weren't afraid of the noises we heard at night. What a superb way for my father to prepare us for our time in the woods!

In the same way, believers need help developing their spiritual senses, which are given to them by God. It is crucial to their development and their later usefulness to God. The local church is a major factor in that type of development, as are the believers God places around the new believers at spiritual birth.

Each child of God must learn to hear and recognize the voice of God and to obey Him. Jesus assured us that His followers, His sheep, would be able to hear His voice, recognize it, and follow (obey) Him:

> "But he who enters by the door is the shepherd of the sheep. To him the doorkeeper opens, and the sheep hear his voice; and he calls his own sheep by name and leads them out. And when he brings out his own sheep, he goes before them; and the sheep follow him, for they know his voice.". . .
>
> "My sheep hear My voice, and I know them, and they follow Me."
>
> —JOHN 10:2–4, 27

Are you coming to sense the personal nature of your relationship with Christ, which began when He called you? As you mature in this relationship and develop your spiritual senses, you will come to hear, recognize, and understand the voice of God as He seeks to use your life for His purposes.

Let's summarize:

✓ **Each child of God must be given spiritual senses in order to "see" the activity of God and join Him.**

Jesus answered and said to him, "Most assuredly, I say to you, unless one is born again, he cannot see the kingdom of God."

—JOHN 3:3

✓ **A servant sees where the Master is working and joins Him.**

"If anyone serves Me, let him follow Me; and where I am, there My servant will be also. If anyone serves Me, him My Father will honor."

—JOHN 12:26

But Jesus answered them, "My Father has been working until now, and I have been working."

—JOHN 5:17

✓ **The servant does not take the initiative; the Master does.**

Then Jesus answered and said to them, "Most assuredly, I say to you, the Son can do nothing of Himself, but what He sees the Father do; for whatever He does, the Son also does in like manner. For the Father loves the Son, and shows Him all things that He Himself does; and He will show Him greater works than these, that you may marvel."

—JOHN 5:19–20

✓ **The servant has died to self and come alive to his Lord.**

"Most assuredly, I say to you, he who hears My word and believes in Him who sent Me has everlasting life, and shall not come into judgment, but has passed from death into life. Most assuredly, I say to you, the hour is coming, and now is, when the dead will hear the voice of the Son of God; and those who hear will live."

—JOHN 12:24–25

✓ **Every believer must learn to listen to the Holy Spirit with his or her heart and to obey Him.**

"But the Helper, the Holy Spirit, whom the Father will send in My name, He will teach you all things, and bring to your remembrance all things that I said to you."

—JOHN 14:26

"However, when He, the Spirit of truth, has come, He will guide you into all truth; for He will not speak on His own authority, but whatever He hears He will speak; and He will tell you things to come. He will glorify Me, for He will take of what is Mine and declare it to you. All things that the Father has are Mine. Therefore I said that He will take of Mine and declare it to you."

—JOHN 16:13–15

✓ **As believers learn to see and hear from the heavenly Father, they will be able to know clearly what He is telling them to do.**

> *"But he who enters by the door is the shepherd of the sheep. To him the doorkeeper opens, and the sheep hear his voice; and he calls his own sheep by name and leads them out."*
>
> —JOHN 10:2–3

God is always looking at the heart, for out of the heart the entire life proceeds (Mark 7:14–23; Proverbs 4:23). Every sheep that is a part of the Shepherd's flock knows His voice and follows Him. Other sheep in the same fold can assist the lambs as they learn this skill. But you must develop your spiritual senses (Hebrews 5:13–14).

> *Every sheep that is a part of the Shepherd's flock knows His voice and follows Him. Other sheep in the same fold can assist the lambs as they learn this skill.*

As a child is fully equipped with physical senses to function in the physical world, so also is the Christian given spiritual senses to function in the spiritual world in his or her relationship with God. Our spiritual senses help us to hear His voice and follow Him; to see His activity and join Him; and to have hearts that understand and obey Him.

> *"But why do you call Me 'Lord, Lord,' and do not do the things which I say? Whoever comes to Me, and hears My sayings and does them, I will show you whom he is like: He is like a man building a house, who dug deep and laid the foundation on the rock. And when the flood arose, the stream*

beat vehemently against that house, and could not shake it, for it was founded on the rock. But he who heard and did nothing is like a man who built a house on the earth without a foundation, against which the stream beat vehemently; and immediately it fell. And the ruin of that house was great."

—LUKE 6:46–49

Just as a little child learns to function in our world a little at a time, if we are faithful in a little, He will give us more (Luke 16:10). Jesus said when we hear and then obey, we are like a man building his house on a rock—nothing can shake it or destroy it (Luke 6:46–49).

The principles discussed in this section are some things that must be firmly in place in the Christian's life to experience the fullness of God's calling.

PRAYER & APPLICATION

As children of God, we are expected to go on to maturity. Part of our maturing is growing in the ability to hear, recognize, and see God and His activity. How have you been developing your spiritual senses? In which areas are you seeing growth and in which areas do you think you need to be strengthened in your life?

Have you released your life to God so He can use you to help others grow in your church, neighborhood, or workplace? Ask God to show you how He wants to use you to help others grow, and write in your spiritual journal the name of any specific person God places on your heart to encourage.

ACCOUNTABILITY TO GOD REQUIRES OBEDIENCE

Just as simply as a little child, you must daily believe Him. That is, *"He who comes to God must believe that He is, and that He is a rewarder of those who diligently seek Him"* (Hebrews 11:6b). This is because *"without faith it is impossible to please Him"* (Hebrews 11:6a). Therefore, the believer must accept as true all God has revealed about Himself, especially in Scripture, and accept as binding upon his life all He has said, asked, or commanded.

FROM NORMAN: TEACHING OUR CHILDREN TO OBEY US

Dana and I have three beautiful children. As we set out to give guidance and direction to them, one of our goals was to teach them to obey our voices. While they were younger, we practiced this with them in a variety of ways until they understood to obey simple commands immediately. We knew if we taught them to obey our voices, then they would, in turn, be able to obey God's voice as they came to know Him. As they have grown in their knowledge of God, they have all three expressed, at different times, things God has said to them. It brings us great joy when they share, "God is telling me to…" As we walk with them each day, we adjust schedules and events to make sure they have the full opportunity to obey what God is telling them to do. We don't have a lot of rules in our home; in fact, we really have only one: obey Mom and Dad.

With all the heart, mind, soul, and strength, a child of God loves Him and, therefore, trusts Him and responds unconditionally to Him. Paul did this in his life and discovered and bore witness that the love of Christ constrained (compelled) him (2 Corinthians 5:14).

Paul expressed his deep sense of accountability to God throughout much of his writing. For example, in 2 Corinthians 5:11, we read these words: *"Knowing, therefore, the terror of the Lord, we persuade men; but we are well known to God, and I also trust are well known in your consciences."*

Paul also said that when he was saved, God not only reconciled him to Himself, but committed to him and all believers *"the ministry of reconciliation"*:

> *Now all things are of God, who has reconciled us to Himself through Jesus Christ, and has given us the ministry of reconciliation . . . . Now then, we are ambassadors for Christ, as though God were pleading through us: we implore you on Christ's behalf, be reconciled to God.*
>
> —2 Corinthians 5:18, 20

Jesus had clearly indicated to His disciples that there will be a time of accountability with God (see Matthew 25). It will be a serious time before God. And He will reward everyone according to his faithful obedience to the Master. Each will hear his Lord and Master say, *"Well done, good and faithful servant; you have been faithful over a few things, I will make you ruler over many things. Enter into the joy of your lord"* (Matthew 25:23).

As you read the following passages, notice Paul's sense of accountability and urgency to honor God in the call He had placed on his life.

> *But by the grace of God I am what I am, and His grace toward me was not in vain; but I labored more abundantly than they all, yet not I, but the grace of God which was with me.*
>
> —1 CORINTHIANS 5:10

> *And whatever you do in word or deed, do all in the name of the Lord Jesus, giving thanks to God the Father through Him. . . .*
>
> *And whatever you do, do it heartily, as to the Lord and not to men, knowing that from the Lord you will receive the reward of the inheritance; for you serve the Lord Christ.*
>
> —COLOSSIANS 3:17, 23–24

It is certainly clear that our accountability is not just at the Judgment, but in this life also. As we are faithful in a little, He gives us more. This truth is illustrated vividly in Jesus's parable of the talents:

"For the kingdom of heaven is like a man traveling to a far country, who called his own servants and delivered his goods to them. And to one he gave five talents, to another two, and to another one, to each according to his own ability; and immediately he went on a journey. Then he who had received the five talents went and traded with them, and made another five talents. And likewise he who had received two gained two more also. But he who had received one went and dug in the ground, and hid his lord's money. After a long time the lord of those servants came and settled accounts with them. So he who had received five talents came and brought five other talents, saying, 'Lord, you delivered to me five talents; look, I have gained five more talents besides them.' His lord said to him, 'Well done, good and faithful servant; you were faithful over a few things, I will make you ruler over many things. Enter into the joy of your lord.' He also who had received two talents came and said, 'Lord, you delivered to me two talents; look, I have gained two more talents besides them.' His lord said to him, 'Well done, good and faithful servant; you have been faithful over a few things, I will make you ruler over many things. Enter into the joy of your lord.' Then he who had received the one talent came and said, 'Lord, I knew you to be a hard man, reaping where you have not sown, and gathering where you have not scattered seed. And I was afraid, and went and hid your talent in the ground. Look, there you have what is yours.' But his lord answered and said to him, 'You wicked and lazy servant, you knew that I reap where I have not sown, and gather where I have not scattered seed. So you ought to have deposited my money with the bankers, *and at my coming I would have received back my own with interest. Therefore take the talent from him, and give it to him who has ten talents. For to everyone who has, more will be given, and he will have abundance; but from him who does not have, even what he has will be taken away. And cast the unprofitable servant into the outer darkness. There will be weeping and gnashing of teeth.'"*

—MATTHEW 25:14–30

To live without a real sense of accountability is to lose a major motivation in serving our Lord! Just to know that not a thing we do goes without His notice and love brings comfort. To love Him with all the heart, soul, mind, and strength brings with it such an intimate relationship and spontaneous, joyful accountability. All those who have been greatly used of God lived this way.

> *To live without a real sense of accountability is to lose a major motivation in serving our Lord!*

Obedience is a by-product of your accountability to God. As you grow in your accountability to your Lord, you will unhesitatingly and immediately obey Him. Jesus said, *"If anyone loves me, he will obey my teaching. My Father will love him, and we will come to him and make our home with him. He who does not love me will not obey my teaching"* (John 14:23–24 NIV).

The Holy Spirit, your enabler, will assist you in hearing, knowing, and doing the call and will of God. He will do this all through your life.

Let's take a moment to read several Scriptures that describe the roles of the Holy Spirit in helping you to follow God's call on your life.

Teacher: *"But the Helper, the Holy Spirit, whom the Father will send in My name, He will teach you all things, and bring to your remembrance all things that I said to you"* (John 14:26).

Giver of God's Love: *"And not only that, but we also glory in tribulations, knowing that tribulation produces perseverance; and perseverance, character; and character, hope. Now hope does not disappoint, because the love of God has been poured out in our hearts by the Holy Spirit who was given to us"* (Romans 5:3–5).

Interceder: *"Likewise the Spirit also helps in our weaknesses. For we do not know what we should pray for as we ought, but the Spirit Himself makes intercession for us with groanings which cannot be uttered"* (Romans 8:26).

Revealer of God's Will: *"But God has revealed them to us through His Spirit. For the Spirit searches all things, yes, the deep things of God"* (1 Corinthians 2:10).

Speaker: *"However, when He, the Spirit of truth, has come, He will guide you into all truth; for He will not speak on His own authority, but whatever He hears He will speak; and He will tell you things to come. He will glorify Me, for He will take of what is Mine and declare it to you. All things that the Father has are Mine. Therefore I said that He will take of Mine and declare it to you"* (John 16:13–15).

Command Giver: *"Then the Spirit told me to go with them, doubting nothing. Moreover these six brethren accompanied me, and we entered the man's house"* (Acts 11:12).

Forbidder: *"Now when they had gone through Phrygia and the region of Galatia, they were forbidden by the Holy Spirit to preach the word in Asia"* (Acts 16:6).

Reprover: *"And when He has come, He will convict the world of sin, and of righteousness, and of judgment"* (John 16:8).

Leader: *"For as many as are led by the Spirit of God, these are sons of God"* (Romans 8:14).

Messenger: *"He who has an ear, let him hear what the Spirit says to the churches"* (Revelation 2:7).

It is encouraging to know that as we obey God and His call on our lives, the Holy Spirit has been assigned to assist us in honoring God. Often we can get discouraged or afraid when we see the assignment ahead of us. However, it is important to realize that we are only instructed to follow one step at a time and be concerned with one day at a time. Remember that Jesus has warned us not to worry about tomorrow (Matthew 6:34), but simply take each day and turn it over to the Lord.

> *It is within the church family that the spiritual atmosphere is created in which the ordinary Christian can hear the call of God and respond confidently.*

For example, you may be sensing that God is calling you to teach the Bible to others (which we have already learned is a sign of maturing in Christ), but you may never have taught or led in the church before. God will not simply thrust you into ministry without preparing your life first. He may provide an opportunity to share at a Bible study or share a testimony at church first. He may place you in a class with a teacher who will mentor you and help you know how to study and share the truths of God. Remember that God is faithful to prepare you for the assignment that He calls you to do.

Furthermore, it is within the church family that the spiritual atmosphere is created in which the ordinary Christian can hear the call of God and respond confidently. Here, the call of God is clarified, and the Christian is assisted in obeying God's call.

The missions organizations of the church have a key role in creating this spiritual atmosphere, so every believer can experience his or her calling and carry it out in a responsible, effective way. Missions organizations provide opportunities for Bible study, mission study, missions activities, personal involvement,

It is in the midst of serving our Lord that His call is clarified.

models for missions, and ministry and service opportunities. It is in the midst of serving our Lord that His call is clarified. When His call is clarified, we can respond with obedience!

FROM NORMAN: A BIBLE STUDY WITH GOLFERS

Matt has become a very good friend of mine over the years, although I don't remember the first time we met. His wife and my wife were a part of a Bible study group and Matt was not involved in church during that time. After years of being prayed for by his wife and others, he turned his life over to the Lord. From that moment on, his life was radically different. A few months ago, Matt called to ask for my advice. You see Matt is a golf pro and works at two golf courses in the Atlanta area. He often teaches golf lessons, and one day he began to sense that God wanted to use his golf to bring lost people to Himself. Matt prayed and released his life to do whatever God wanted him to do. After a few weeks, a group of his students came to him and asked him to start a Bible study after their weekly golf lessons.

Matt knew that this was God's invitation, so he obeyed. While he wasn't as comfortable teaching the Bible as he was teaching golf, he came to love it. Matt could have asked a pastor from his church to lead the Bible study, but God was calling him to do it. He left his comfort zone and obeyed.

FROM HENRY: THE HOW OF BEING CALLED

Linda and Renee came to our association as volunteer missionaries. They had sensed the call of God to come and spend two years with us. During those two years, we sought to create a spiritual atmosphere in which God would have the maximum opportunity to reveal to each of them the next step in His claim on and call for their lives. We spent time in Bible study and answering questions. They were given assignments that they sensed were from the Lord, and they responded eagerly. We walked with them through the disappointments, failures, victories, and the painful and happy times.

When their assignments ended, Renee went on to other missions assignments and on to seminary training in preparation for a life of ministry. Linda went on to direct the Southern Baptist witness to the Winter Olympics in Calgary, Alberta, and then to serve in New York and Atlanta; she is now ministering in Alaska with her Lord. What began as two-year assignments brought them each into the relationship of obedience that turned into a lifetime of ministry.

The how of being called of God came for both Renee and Linda in the midst of their personal relationship with God and His people as they followed their Lord daily.

Prayer & Application

Everything in the Christian's life rests on obedience! Obedience always unlocks the activity of God in a Christian's life. Obedience is where all the real activity of God on mission begins. Obedience is the essential heart of experiencing a life on mission with God in the world.

Is your obedience to God unlocking the activity of God in and through your life? Are there areas of your life that you have not fully surrendered to God—areas in which you have not obeyed Him? Spend some time before the Lord and ask Him if you have been faithful to obey all He has been asking you to do. Write down what God tells you about your obedience to Him and His claim on your life.

Rebecca

Putting Aside Her Fears

Rebecca was a very shy person—so shy that she hardly spoke in her college Sunday School class. After graduating from college, she felt God was calling her to be an adult sponsor for a World Changers group. She was assigned to drive a group of young people around for the week. Because of her shyness, she was very afraid to go and wanted to back out.

Many of her friends surrounded her and prayed for her the night before she was scheduled to leave. Finally, she realized that God had called her to go on the trip and that she needed to put aside her fears and trust God. She stepped out in faith, and as a result, God radically changed Rebecca's life.

Upon returning home, she felt led to apply for a short-term missions assignment. She was accepted and assigned to East Asia, where her job was to build relationships and teach English. As she built relationships at the school, over the Christmas season, the school asked her to explain Western culture by reading the Christmas story over the loudspeaker to the entire campus. Rebecca was amazed at how much fun she had serving the Lord in a foreign land.

When the assignment ended, she returned home and sensed a call into full-time Christian service. She is now serving as a career missionary in East Asia. Rebecca's life of service to the Lord and living out God's call on her life began when she set aside her fears and stepped out in faith, believing her Lord would take care of her. The trust that the Lord built in her heart with a small assignment of driving a vanload of youth has blossomed into an incredible journey of service to her Lord.

CHAPTER 5

When Am I Called?

ESSENTIAL TRUTH

God is God! When He speaks, He also ensures that you will hear and will know His call. Your heart will be revealed in your response to Him.

> "No one can come to Me unless the Father who sent Me draws him; and I will raise him up at the last day."
>
> —JOHN 6:44

> "He who has My commandments and keeps them, it is he who loves Me. And he who loves Me will be loved by My Father, and I will love him and manifest Myself to him."
>
> —JOHN 14:21

> "If anyone loves Me, he will keep My word; and My Father will love him, and We will come to him and make Our home with him."
>
> —JOHN 14:23

> "However, when He, the Spirit of truth, has come, He will guide you into all truth; for He will not speak on His own authority, but whatever He hears He will speak; and He will tell you things to come. He will glorify Me, for He will take of what is Mine and declare it to you."
>
> —JOHN 16:13–14

Melvin and Carrie Wells

Testimony from Henry Blackaby About His Wife's Parents

Melvin worked for Sears for many years. Carrie was a nurse. They served faithfully in their church. He served as a deacon and Sunday School director; she taught youth and was actively involved with Woman's Missionary Union® in her church and association of churches. Melvin was a "natural salesman" (as demonstrated on the job at Sears) and soon was in charge of promoting the Bible Way correspondence courses. Over the years, he enrolled tens of thousands of people into the course, many of whom became Christians. He also was given oversight of a church to give counsel to the deacons and leaders.

In their late 50s, Melvin and Carrie were called by God to use the rest of their lives in missions overseas. They immediately applied to the Foreign Mission Board (now the International Mission Board) and were appointed as missionary associates to Zambia, where they served faithfully for the next several years. Together, Melvin and Carrie became houseparents for missionary children. Melvin helped build the residences, and Carrie became an adopted mother to them all.

In the midst of these ordinary lives that God used, all three of their children became involved in missions too. Their eldest daughter spent years with her husband in Eastern Europe (before the Berlin Wall came down) and at a seminary in Switzerland; their other daughter, my wife, Marilynn, served in Canada with me in church planting; and their son served in Singapore and is now teaching at a seminary in Canada.

Melvin and Carrie were ordinary people who recognized a clear call from God, obeyed immediately, and were used of God, even in their "later" years.

KNOWING THE CALL

As we carefully study the lives of those God used significantly, the Bible reveals that it is when we are in the middle of God's activity in our world that we most clearly know the call of God for our lives. A key verse that helps us understand this is found in the life and witness of Jesus.

> But Jesus answered them, "My Father has been working until now, and I have been working." ... Then Jesus answered and said to them, "Most assuredly, I say to you, the Son can do nothing of Himself, but what He sees the Father do; for whatever He does, the Son also does in like manner. For the Father loves the Son, and shows Him all things that He Himself does; and He will show Him greater works than these, that you may marvel."
>
> —JOHN 5:17, 19–20

According to this Scripture, select the correct answer(s) for the following questions:

What did Jesus say He was doing when the Father revealed His plan?
- ❏ Waiting anxiously
- ❏ Pouting, being disillusioned
- ❏ Already working

Why does the Father show the Son what He is doing?

❑ To confuse Him

❑ Because the Father loves the Son and so the Son can join Him in His work

❑ To show Him a better way

When the Father reveals what He is doing, how does Jesus respond?

❑ Does nothing

❑ Acknowledges Him, but continues "business as usual"

❑ Immediately joins the Father in His work

First, Jesus said that it was the Father who was at work in the world. Jesus was His chosen servant. Jesus said the Son (servant) does not take the initiative, but rather watches to see where the Father (Master) is working and joins Him. Jesus said the Father loves the Son, and therefore shows Him everything that He Himself is doing. The Son joins in with the Father, working together with Him. It is then that the Father is able to complete all He has purposed to do through the Son. This is how God purposed to bring a lost world back to Himself. He does it through His Son, who loves, trusts, and obeys the Father.

This same pattern is true for how the Father involves Christians in His work today. Because of the relationship of love between the Father and Christians, He will show them where He is working. When He shows us His work, we must be quick to join Him and, in turn, become workers together with Christ.

The example of the life of Christ shows it may be costly to join God as He reveals His work. Yet the end results always glorify God and His purposes. Notice what the Scriptures say concerning the enormous price God and His Son paid for this great salvation.

Who, in the days of His flesh, when He had offered up prayers and supplications, with vehement cries and tears to Him who was able to save Him from death, and was heard because of His godly fear, though He was a Son, yet He learned obedience by the things which He suffered. And having been perfected, He became the author of eternal salvation to all who obey Him.

—HEBREWS 5:7–9

What was the end result of Jesus joining God when the Father revealed His activity? It cost Jesus His life!

Every person through whom God is able to work mightily lives out this kind of relationship with God.

Amos, the prophet, was a layman (shepherd and caretaker of sycamore-fig trees). He said:

"I was no prophet,
Nor was I a son of a prophet,

But I was a sheepbreeder
And a tender of sycamore fruit.
Then the LORD *took me as I followed the flock,*
And the LORD *said to me,*
'Go, prophesy to My people Israel.' "

—AMOS 7:14–15

God had an urgent message that His people, Israel, needed to hear immediately! Time was running out for them. Judgment was very near. God wanted them to hear from Him about His love one more time. Amos was the man God chose to take His message to His people. It surprised Amos, but he responded obediently, and God accomplished His purposes through him. Though they did not heed His message, they knew God had spoken to them through Amos.

> *The safest place you and your family can be is in the center of God's will.*

Have you ever felt like Amos when he said, "I *was no prophet, nor was I a son of a prophet*"? Often we quote the first part of Amos's words but do not follow through with the obedience of Amos. If God has called you, obey immediately! The safest place you and your family can be is in the center of God's will.

God also called and used Jeremiah in a similar way. Though the pattern is very similar, the messenger is different. Listen to what happened:

Then the word of the LORD came to me, saying:
"Before I formed you in the womb I knew you;
Before you were born I sanctified you;
I ordained you a prophet to the nations."
Then said I:
"Ah, Lord GOD!
Behold, I cannot speak, for I am a youth."
But the LORD said to me:
"Do not say, 'I am a youth,'
For you shall go to all to whom I send you,
And whatever I command you, you shall speak.
Do not be afraid of their faces,
For I am with you to deliver you," says the LORD.
Then the LORD put forth His hand and touched my mouth,
and the LORD said to me:
"Behold, I have put My words in your mouth.
See, I have this day set you over the nations and over the
kingdoms,
To root out and to pull down,
To destroy and to throw down,
To build and to plant."
Moreover the word of the LORD came to me, saying,
"Jeremiah, what do you see?" And I said, "I see a branch
of an almond tree."
Then the LORD said to me, "You have seen well, for I am
ready to perform My word."

—JEREMIAH 1:4–12

Have you ever felt like Jeremiah and stated, "I am only a youth and cannot speak or stand before the people"? God is not looking for all of your qualifications or abilities; He is looking for your obedience. He will give you the words, the opportunities, and the ability, but He wants you to give Him your heart—that is, your trust, faith, and willingness to serve.

God wanted to speak clearly and forcefully to His people, Judah and Jerusalem, and He chose Jeremiah to be His spokesperson. But the heart of God knew long before Jeremiah was even born that He had set him apart for this important time in history. This time was critical for His people. God wanted both a long and a passionate pleading from His heart to come to His people. Jeremiah was then shaped by God to be the one through whom He would speak. So tender was the message to Judah that Jeremiah was called the weeping prophet!

God has found messengers through whom He could speak and work in every generation in history. One well-known messenger was Moses:

> Moreover God said to Moses, "Thus you shall say to the children of Israel: 'The Lord God of your fathers, the God of Abraham, the God of Isaac, and the God of Jacob, has sent me to you. This is My name forever, and this is My memorial to all generations.'"
>
> —Exodus 3:15

Other notable messengers chosen by God include the judges, David, all the prophets, the disciples, and the Apostle Paul; many more of God's people throughout history have been chosen by God for a specific work. This God-chosen process continues to this very day and is the way God will call and work through your life too. God has worked and moved throughout history to accomplish His eternal purpose. Always, eternity is in the balance. Those He chooses, calls, shapes, and uses are painfully and deeply aware of this "assignment." They are the clay and God is the potter. God always has a design in mind when He chooses a person.

Has God called you to an assignment in which you have felt inadequate to serve? Have you made excuses that have kept you from obeying?

As we walk with the Lord, we must not forget that God will be shaping and molding us for His purposes. When God puts a deep accountability on your heart to serve Him, make sure you recognize God's shaping hand on your life with His current desire to use your life.

Hopefully by now you are coming to understand that God wants only your heart and availability to Him. He can and will shape you for the assignment, but He needs you to step out and allow Him access to fashion your life for use in His eternal plan. Those God chooses and calls know it is God, know what He is saying, and know how they are to release their lives to Him for His purposes in their day!

Prayer & Application

Read the following passage from Jeremiah 18 to see how God desires to shape a life for His service. List some of your discoveries in your spiritual journal.

> *The word which came to Jeremiah from the LORD, saying: "Arise and go down to the potter's house, and there I will cause you to hear My words." Then I went down to the potter's house, and there he was, making something at the wheel. And the vessel that he made of clay was marred in the hand of the potter; so he made it again into another vessel, as it seemed good to the potter to make. Then the word of the LORD came to me, saying: "O house of Israel, can I not do with you as this potter?" says the LORD. "Look, as the clay is in the potter's hand, so are you in My hand, O house of Israel!"*
>
> —JEREMIAH 18:1–6

Based on this Scripture, can you see how God has been shaping your life with His hands? Explain in your spiritual journal how God has been molding your life recently. What assignment are you deeply aware of that God has given you in the last month? How have you released your life to be used for His purposes?

A Daily Walk, Thoroughly Rearranged

When God sees in one of His children a growing, loving, and responsive relationship of trust in Him, He continues His call on that person's life. He usually does this in the midst of a person's daily routine. Through this daily routine, God calls a person to a special and deeper relationship with Him. It is also remarkable that the daily response of each person brings the enabling presence and power of the Spirit of God closer to being accomplished through a person's assignment with God.

For example, God placed His Spirit on the responsive Moses and, later, on the 70 elders who were to work with him (Numbers 11:16–25). Moses's daily walk with God, guiding God's people, was exceedingly demanding for Moses. It required the full presence and enabling that only the Spirit of God could bring. But God also provided 70 other key leaders to share this leadership load. In their new assignments, they would require the same Spirit of God. God provided thoroughly and adequately for them all. This enabling provided what was needed for the leaders to guide God's people according to His commands and purposes.

Has God placed able people in your life to walk alongside of you as a source of help and encouragement? If so, write in your journal their names and how God is using them to strengthen your life. If not, make this a matter of prayer until God brings some of His people around you to walk with you.

As I served alongside my dad at Blackaby Ministries, my job was very lonely at times, because we had relatively few persons on staff and they were often scattered across two countries. However, God provided a solution for the loneliness. One of my responsibilities was to write and teach online classes for our ministry. We taught more than 30 classes, and many people took the classes every time they were offered. Through these friendships, God gave Dana and me friends from around the world to walk with us and encourage us each day. To this day, two of Dana's closest prayer partners live more than 1,000 miles from us, but Dana maintains intimate friendships with these two through the carrying of each other's burdens. God may have you serving in a missions environment where you don't have a close Christian friend to pray with or talk to each day. I encourage you to ask God to give you a friend you could pray with from another part of the world. With all the technology in our day, communication is quick and easy.

After some of Moses's leadership responsibilities had been delegated, God commanded Moses to build a tabernacle for His presence among His people. It would require the utmost care and obedience to all God would direct. God told Moses He had already chosen and placed His Spirit on some men who would do all that He commanded. They were ordinary workmen, chosen by God and equipped by God's Spirit to do His will in all things. As you read the following passage from Exodus, notice the kind of work God equipped the people to do.

> And Moses said to the children of Israel, "See, the LORD has called by name Bezalel the son of Uri, the son of Hur, of the tribe of Judah; and He has filled him with the Spirit of God, in wisdom and understanding, in knowledge and all manner of workmanship, to design artistic works, to work in gold and silver and bronze, in cutting jewels for setting, in carving wood, and to work in all manner of artistic workmanship. And He has put in his heart the ability to teach, in him and Aholiab the son of Ahisamach, of the tribe of Dan. He has filled them with skill to do all manner of work of the engraver and the designer and the tapestry maker, in blue, purple, and scarlet thread, and fine linen, and of the weaver—those who do every work and those who design artistic works. And Bezalel and Aholiab, and every gifted artisan in whom the LORD has put wisdom and understanding, to know how to do all manner of work for the service of the sanctuary, shall do according to all that the LORD has commanded."
>
> —EXODUS 35:30 THROUGH 36:1

Do you find it surprising that the Spirit equipped them to do all manner of work—building, wood carving, artistic works, tapestry making, and weaving? Often we assume that the Spirit equips people only to preach or teach the gospel. However, God equips His people in a wide range of talents to be used to bring honor to

His name. For example, many retired laypeople are being called of God to use their trade skills to build churches, repair buildings after disasters, and renovate church camps. To watch these people work and hear their heart for God is to know that they have been anointed by God for His service. Many times the wives of these workmen bring along sewing machines and make clothes for children in need. When you see their work, it becomes clear that Exodus 35:35—*"He has filled them with skill to do all manner of work"*—is actively demonstrated throughout their lives and ministries.

> *God equips His people in a wide range of talents to be used to bring honor to His name.*

This pattern of God working through ordinary people, called, assigned, and enabled by God, continued through each of the judges of Israel. Each was called at a crucial moment in the life of God's people when they needed deliverance from their enemies. David's life follows this same pattern (1 Samuel 16:13); the disciples and the Apostle Paul were also shaped and used by God in their day.

Now it is our turn. This is especially true because God has huge purposes to accomplish through His people in our generation. Our world is changing, and God is orchestrating His people to accomplish His purposes. But oftentimes, they are not in a spiritual condition to respond to Him! So once again, God is looking for someone who will stand in the gap before Him on behalf of the land, that He should not destroy it (see Ezekiel 22:30).

So much is in the balance, especially eternally. The heart of God has not changed. He is *"not willing that any should perish, but that all should come to repentance"* (2 Peter 3:9). So in this our day and in your life and mine, the following is still incredibly true:

> *"For the eyes of the LORD run to and fro throughout the whole earth, to show Himself strong on behalf of those whose heart is loyal to Him."*
>
> —2 CHRONICLES 16:9

The key to being used by God is the condition of our hearts and our willingness to respond in obedience to His call on our lives. Our usefulness to God does not lie in our abilities or talents or in the lack of them, but in our availability. So the process continues. But now, it involves you, and it involves me! And God is watching to see how we will respond to Him.

PRAYER & APPLICATION

Why is the condition of a person's heart and not one's abilities the basis on which God chooses to use a person? Spend some before God asking Him to show you how He sees your heart: Is it totally willing and available?

COMPLETELY ENABLED

The one God calls, He thoroughly and completely equips to enable that one to respond in every matter toward God.

God is on mission and the servant of the Lord must be where the Master is. Jesus said, *"If anyone serves Me, let him follow Me; and where I am, there My servant will be also"* (John 12:26a). And Jesus added, significantly, *"If anyone serves Me, him My Father will honor"* (v. 26b). Whole books could be written just on this intimate relationship between the Lord and His servants.

> *God is on mission and the servant of the Lord must be where the Master is.*

This closeness, this proximity with the Master, is needed for the called to receive the provision. The enabling provision of God for His servants is clearly declared and seen throughout Scripture and history. Some of the provisions of God are clear. For example, we know Paul's words in Philippians 4:19: *"And my God shall supply all your need according to His riches in glory by Christ Jesus."* Did you notice how many of your needs God promises to supply?

In 2 Corinthians 1:20, Paul reminds us that *"all the promises of God in Him [Jesus Christ] are Yes, and in Him Amen, to the glory of God through us."* And in 2 Peter 1:3–4, we hear such an encouraging message: *"His divine power has given to us all things that pertain to life and godliness, through the knowledge of Him who called us by glory and virtue, by which have been given to us exceedingly great and precious promises, that through these you may be partakers of the divine nature, having escaped the corruption that is in the world through lust."* If we were to take each phrase of these verses to heart, we would have absolutely no room for worry or fretting, no room for complaining or for feeling inadequate in our Christian lives, no room for laziness or depression. God's provisions are perfect and always on time for His children.

The greatest of God's provisions is His Holy Spirit. Jesus assured His disciples, *"You shall receive power when the Holy Spirit has come upon you"* (Acts 1:8). He had earlier told them, *"I will pray the Father, and He will give you another Helper, that He may abide with you forever—the Spirit of truth"* (John 14:16–17). He (the Holy Spirit) would always let the believers know the Father's will for each of them (John 16:13; 1 Corinthians 2:9–16). He would guide them into all truth, teach them all things, and bring to their remembrance everything Christ had commanded them (John 16:13–15; John 14:26). He would also help them when they prayed (Romans 8:26), an activity that would be so much a part of their relationship with God and His will in their lives. And the Holy Spirit would work the Scriptures into their lives as a *"sword"* (Ephesians 6:17).

Those God used in the Old Testament had the Spirit come upon them to totally enable them. In the New Testament, every believer would have the Spirit of God at conversion. But more significantly, the Holy Spirit would "fill" those whom God called to be available to Him as He took His great salvation message to the whole world.

Now, once again, it is our turn. All that was available to people in the Scriptures is available today to every believer called of God. The Holy Spirit is God Himself, present and active, enabling every believer to do whatever God commands. No matter what it is that God commands the believer to do with Him, His provision is already present and available, and the Holy Spirit is actively working to implement all of it into that believer's life. No matter how difficult or impossible an assignment God places on the life of one of His children, God's provision will completely enable him to do it.

> *All that was available to people in the Scriptures is available today to every believer called of God.*

God's provision for every believer on mission with Him is the fullness of His presence. In His presence, we are *"complete."* Paul describes it this way: *"For in Him dwells all the fullness of the Godhead bodily; and you are complete in Him, who is the head of all principality and power"* (Colossians 2:9–10). Every believer is enabled to experience God finishing His work through them: *"being confident of this very thing, that He who has begun a good work in you will complete it until the day of Jesus Christ"* (Philippians 1:6).

The Holy Spirit does this completing or enabling in many ways. One way of enabling comes as the believer spends time in God's Word. In the midst of the study, the Holy Spirit gives a confirming "Yes" to what He knows to be the will of God. It comes as a quiet assurance, giving peace and joy. He also gives affirmation when the believer takes time to pray and seek assurance from God of His will. To the carefully observant person who prays, there comes a quiet direction to the prayer, putting the person into the center of the will of God (Romans 8:26–28). When John was praying on the island of Patmos, the Holy Spirit gave him clear direction concerning the will of God (Revelation 1).

What affirmations and enabling has God brought to your life from prayer and Bible study this past month? Take a moment to read through your spiritual journal from the past few weeks, and let the Holy Spirit remind you of the words He spoke to you and the things He has revealed to you about your life and service.

Throughout history, the witness of those used of God indicates that some of the great affirmations of God have come to them in prayer. Further affirmations of God come by what He is doing around the believer and in the midst of His people, the local church.

It is important to keep in mind that God can and does affirm His will for His servants. If God does not express Himself toward you, He may be trying to let you know something else. When God promises something, He does it. If you sense you know God's will and, yet, do not see God doing what He promised (Isaiah 46:11b; Isaiah 14:24, 27; 1 Kings 8:56), God may be seeking to tell you that either you are not in His will or that His timing is not always immediate. God may be taking the time necessary to develop character in your life before He can give you all He has planned for you. Ask God and He will guide you to know the truth of your situation.

God has promised incredible affirmation of His will and His call in our lives. It is important that each believer

> God may be seeking to tell you that either you are not in His will or that His timing is not always immediate.

be constantly alert to God's word of confirmation, however He chooses to express it. But never go long without some affirmation from the Lord that you are in the center of His will.

Prayer & Application

Describe how God has confirmed that you are currently in the middle of His will and are faithfully fulfilling His call upon your life.

Necessity of Functioning in the Body

Christians will know more completely when they are being called by God as they function in the life of His church (the body of Christ). The most complete pictures of the body working together are found in 1 Corinthians 12, Ephesians 4, and Romans 12. Each member in the body functions where God places him or her in the body, and each assists the other parts of the body to grow up into the Head, which is Christ. This is not merely a figure of speech; it is a living reality. The loving Christ is truly present in the church body, and each member really does assist the others in knowing and doing the will of God. Paul constantly affirmed his need of other believers to help him know and carry out the call of God in his life.

FROM HENRY: HELPING OTHERS ENCOURAGE THE CHURCH BODY
As I pastored for more than 30 years, I learned to help our church members find their areas of service. One way I did this was by watching to see where a person brought encouragement to the body. For example, if I took someone with me to visit at the hospital and noticed that person always caused the one we were visiting to be uplifted and encouraged, then I would let that person know that God was using his or her life to bring "life and health" to our body. I remember one person who wanted to be an encourager to those in need. However, every time she would visit someone, I would get a phone call with concern from the person she visited. So as I sought the Lord regarding this woman, He showed me that every time this person prayed, we saw immediate answers. So I began to help this woman see that the best way she could encourage our body was to be in prayer.

She was overjoyed to hear this word from me, and God used her prayer life to encourage every part of our church, from the youth to the senior adults.

> *For I long to see you, that I may impart to you some spiritual gift, so that you may be established—that is, that I may be encouraged together with you by the mutual faith both of you and me.*
>
> —ROMANS 1:11–12

> *And [pray] for me, that utterance may be given to me, that I may open my mouth boldly to make known the mystery of the gospel, for which I am an ambassador in chains; that in it I may speak boldly, as I ought to speak.*
>
> —EPHESIANS 6:19–20

How is your life currently encouraging others in their faith in the church you attend? Are you allowing others in your church to encourage you? In the church where God places you, He has provided other believers whom He has equipped to assist you in knowing God's call and activity in your life and whom God has chosen to assist you in carrying out His will.

Your involvement, or activity, in the body of Christ is crucial if God is to carry out His eternal purpose for your life today. The eye can help the ear to know what it is hearing; the hand, to know what it is feeling; and the feet, to know where to step next.

The life of the body is affected by each member relating in love to one another (Ephesians 4:16).

Understanding this will involve you not only in your church family but also with other churches (as happened in the New Testament) in your local area, across the nation, and around the world. God's call is to take the gospel to every person and into every nation. God's plan for accomplishing this is to call you to Himself, and then place your life alongside all the others He has called, so that together, as one people, He can work dramatically across an entire world through His people, you being a part of the whole!

> God's call in your life always includes your intimate involvement with His people in and through your local church.

God's call in your life always includes your intimate involvement with His people in and through your local church.

FROM NORMAN: WAITING FOR GOD'S INVITATION

When God called me to leave the church I was pastoring and move to Atlanta to serve alongside my mom and dad in their new ministry, Dana and I faced many adjustments. One of the most difficult adjustments we faced was shifting from being a senior pastor to being a layperson within a large church. As we began to see where God was leading us, He took us to a Sunday School class with others who were our age. It was a great group of people. We waited to see what assignment God might be giving us in the midst of our transition. Within a few months, the women in the class asked Dana to teach a women's Bible study, and the men asked me to lead a men's accountability group. We were so thankful that we waited on God's invitation! For the next two years, God allowed us to disciple a group of wonderful Christian people, who were growing daily in their love for and obedience to God. Those people have become some our lifelong friends and prayer partners. We are so thankful that we didn't take the initiative to find our own areas of service, but waited for God to reveal His plans for us in that church.

PRAYER & APPLICATION

Read the following passage and prayerfully consider the questions that follow. Record your thoughts in your spiritual journal.

> *I, therefore, the prisoner of the Lord, beseech you to walk worthy of the calling with which you were called, with all lowliness and gentleness, with longsuffering, bearing with one another in love, endeavoring to keep the unity of the Spirit in the bond of peace. There is one body and one Spirit, just as you were called in one hope of your calling; one Lord, one faith, one baptism; one God and Father of all, who is above all, and through all, and in you all. But to each one of us grace was given according to the*

measure of Christ's gift. Therefore He says: "When He ascended on high, He led captivity captive, and gave gifts to men." (Now this, "He ascended"—what does it mean but that He also first descended into the lower parts of the earth? He who descended is also the One who ascended far above all the heavens, that He might fill all things.) And He Himself gave some to be apostles, some prophets, some evangelists, and some pastors and teachers, for the equipping of the saints for the work of ministry, for the edifying of the body of Christ, till we all come to the unity of the faith and of the knowledge of the Son of God, to a perfect man, to the measure of the stature of the fullness of Christ; that we should no longer be children, tossed to and fro and carried about with every wind of doctrine, by the trickery of men, in the cunning craftiness of deceitful plotting, but, speaking the truth in love, may grow up in all things into Him who is the head—Christ—from whom the whole body, joined and knit together by what every joint supplies, according to the effective working by which every part does its share, causes growth of the body for the edifying of itself in love.

—Ephesians 4:1–16

How does God want to use you in the church where He has placed you? Are you allowing Him to use you in this manner?

COMPLETE AFFIRMATION

When you are in a personal relationship with God, He, in love, affirms His presence and His call in your life daily!

The heart that seeks Him, finds Him; the life that asks Him, receives; to the one who knocks, God opens a door (Matthew 7:7–11). God responds to His children, and they know that it is God who is affirming their relationship with Him. It is a living, ongoing relationship of love!

The heart that is earnestly seeking God will daily spend time in His Word. When you do this, the Holy Spirit uses the Word of God like a sword (Ephesians 6:17) to convict you of sin, to lead you into "all truth," to teach you "all things," to bring to your remembrance all that Christ has been saying to you, and to help you thoroughly understand and apply His will and call to your life (John 14:26; 16:7–15).

As you, an earnest seeker, open the Scripture, the Holy Spirit is present and actively seeking to bring you into the will of God. Words suddenly have new meanings and seem to apply directly to your life—and they really do. This is the affirmation of God in your life through the working of the Holy Spirit. The same is true of all Scripture—in particular, the life and teachings of Jesus. But *"all Scripture is given by inspiration of God, and is profitable for doctrine, for reproof, for correction, for instruction in righteousness"* (2 Timothy 3:16). Throughout the entire process, the Holy Spirit *"bears witness with [your] spirit,"* not only that you are a child of God, but also that you are in the center of the will of God (Romans 8:16, 27).

If you have a heart that seeks after God, you will also spend much time in prayer. God has given the Holy Spirit the responsibility to guide you into the will of God as you pray (Romans 8:26–27). Too often, prayers start off quite self-centered and self-focused. If you notice this happening, continue to pray; soon your prayer will change in focus and become God-centered—this is the Holy Spirit at work, according to the will of God. Follow the Spirit's directives immediately and completely.

Sometimes God uses friends or family or persons in your church to give you affirmation for your call.

You may start off praying with anger, even resentment, against someone or some situation. Soon God's love fills your heart, and your prayer changes to expressions of love and blessing. This is God. He has affirmed not only His presence but also His will toward your life. Thank Him and alter everything to follow His directives, for He is ready to bless you greatly!

Sometimes God uses friends or family or persons in your church to give you affirmation for your call. Someone shares a Scripture with you that is the very same Scripture God gave you that morning. This is God's affirmation! A timely phone call or letter comes—again, God's affirmation to your life and call. A caution or even a word of correction becomes God's affirmation not to proceed. Remember that you do not live your Christian life in isolation. You will be living out God's call upon your life alongside the rest of God's people.

FROM HENRY: CONFIRMED BY OTHERS

As I pastored, persons would regularly come to me and share that God had placed burdens on their hearts for the church to begin certain new ministries. Sometimes, I could share and let the person know that God had placed the same burden on my heart for the church. As the pastor, I could not lead out in the ministry, but was praying to see whom God would raise up in the church to lead in this area. It was always a joy to see the look on the person's face when I was able to share that his or her burden was from God and an answer to my prayers!

Other times when a person came to me expressing God's call on his or her life, we would begin to pray and ask God to show us if there were others in the church with the same burden. We knew that if God had spoken to one part of the church body, He would also be speaking to others. Time and time again, we watched God speak through His people to the body. Each time God initiated a new ministry, He faithfully provided all we needed to accomplish His will.

Remember, there are no coincidences in the life wholly yielded to God! God is completely involved in the life of the one He calls to go with Him. But an additional word needs to be shared at this point. If you see no affirming presence of God in your life or ministry, you need to stop and see if, indeed, you may be out of God's will, and He is speaking to you by not giving affirmation to your sin and rebellion or disobedience. It is also important to remember that success, as the world defines it, may not at all be the affirming presence of God. God never leaves His children to guess whether they are walking in the center of His will. He provides plenty of daily assurances!

Prayer & Application

As you have been reading this book, you have been looking at God's call upon your life and His desire to use you in the middle of His activity to redeem the lost of this world. You have been looking at how you are serving in your community, church, and beyond.

What affirmations from God have you received that confirm you are truly seeking and honoring Him? What Scriptures has He used to assure you of your walk with Him?

Vicki Sweetman

A Long Life of Service for God

For many years, Vicki served the Lord alongside her husband, who was a pastor of a church in the Washington, D.C., area. Because of some major health issues, she and her husband moved to the southern United States. Not long after their relocation, he passed away. While Vicki was grieved over the loss of her husband, she knew that God had called both of them into the ministry. She realized that her call had not stopped with her husband's death.

She began to ask the Lord where He would have her serve, and He led her to a large church. She joined the church and began to teach a women's Sunday School class. She became involved in ministering to many of the widows in the church and also became an example to the younger women.

In her 80s now, she continues to travel and speak, encouraging other Christians to remain faithful to the Lord's calling on their lives. Through her years of following the Lord, God has fashioned her into a mighty prayer warrior for her church and family. Recently she was invited to speak at an anniversary celebration for the first church that she and her husband pastored more than 50 years ago. While her health has slowed her down at times, she continues to be faithful to serve her Lord with all of her strength.

CHAPTER 6

How Do I Live Out the Call?

ESSENTIAL TRUTH

God's provisions for a relationship with Him are completely thorough. Nothing is missing from God's perspective. God doesn't want us to miss His calling. All through the Scriptures, we see God speaking to His people and their response of obedience or disobedience. What would it take to miss His calling? You would have to resist, quench, and grieve Him, His Son, and His Holy Spirit to miss His call.

For it is God who works in you both to will and to do for His good pleasure.

—PHILIPPIANS 2:13

Clay and Lois Quattlebaum

Serving in Retirement

Clay and Lois first met in university as they were studying to become schoolteachers. Both of them were committed Christians, and they served God faithfully for many years as elementary school teachers in the Southern California public schools. Marilynn and I (Henry) had been friends with Clay and Lois since university. In fact, Lois was a bridesmaid in our wedding. We kept in touch over the years and had always enjoyed their friendship.

Upon retirement, they sensed that God had a new assignment for their lives and ministry. As they prayed for several months, God began to reveal His plans to them. God was inviting them to come and serve alongside Marilynn and me at Blackaby Ministries. This invitation from God required them to make major adjustments. As we prayed together and became convinced that this was God's will, Lois and Clay sold their home in Southern California and relocated to Atlanta to work as volunteers with Blackaby Ministries. This step of obedience caused them to leave a very comfortable retirement, many lifelong friends, and a church family they had been a part of for more than 40 years.

As they have been serving God alongside us for several years, their servant hearts and their willingness to help have brought great joy to us and countless others. If you were to ask them why they left everything that was familiar to them and moved across the country to serve as volunteers, they would say, "Retirement from the public schools didn't mean retirement from serving our Lord!"

DESIRE TO FOLLOW THE CALL

God Himself places within the heart of every believer the deepest desire to experience the strong presence and power of God working in and through that believer. God will not override a believer's heart or will, but He will thoroughly influence that life toward His will and His call. Notice this Scripture passage:

> *Therefore, my beloved, as you have always obeyed, not as in my presence only, but now much more in my absence, work out your own salvation with fear and trembling; for it is God who works in you both to will and to do for His good pleasure.*
>
> —PHILIPPIANS 2:12–13

But how, from the scriptural revelation, do you come to experience in life the deep reality of being called and accountable?

As you look for the answer to this question, it is important to remember that not only does God work in you *"both to will and to do for His good pleasure,"* but also *"He who has begun a good work in you will complete it until the day of Jesus Christ"* (Philippians 1:6). This is a wonderful verse to encourage you to never quit or give up, because God is always faithful to finish the work and complete all He desires to do through your life if you will let Him.

In Paul's letter to the church at Ephesus, he prayed for them that they would not miss out on all that God had provided for them. Certainly this included the wonderful blessing of living out the call of God in their lives as individuals and as a church family.

To better understand this truth, let's carefully examine Paul's prayer found in Ephesians 3:14–21. As you read, remember he specifically prays that God would grant all of these things *"according to the riches of His glory."* Notice all of the different things Paul asked God to give, or grant, to the Ephesian church.

> *For this reason I bow my knees to the Father of our Lord Jesus Christ, from whom the whole family in heaven and earth is named, that He would grant you, according to the riches of His glory, to be strengthened with might through His Spirit in the inner man, that Christ may dwell in your hearts through faith; that you, being rooted and grounded in love, may be able to comprehend with all the saints what is the width and length and depth and height—to know the love of Christ which passes knowledge; that you may be filled with all the fullness of God. Now to Him who is able to do exceedingly abundantly above all that we ask or think, according to the power that works in us, to Him be glory in the church by Christ Jesus to all generations, forever and ever. Amen.*
> —EPHESIANS 3:14–21

Before we study this prayer, it is important to understand the reason Paul prayed this prayer. If we look back to Ephesians 2:19–22, we discover Paul's purpose. In this passage, Paul describes the church as *"fellow citizens with the* saints," "members of the household of God," and "a dwelling place of God in the Spirit." He is reminding them of the radical change that took place in their lives when they received the gift of salvation. Paul is generally saying, "Because of who you are in Christ, I am going to pray these things."

Paul's prayer specifically requests these things:

✓ **The church would be strengthened with might through the Holy Spirit and in the inner man (individually and corporately).**

> How many times do believers struggle to live out the call of God because of a conflict in their hearts? Paul understood this inward struggle, so he prayed that they would rest in God's strength in the very core of who they were—in their hearts.

✓ **Christ would dwell in their hearts through faith.**

> He prayed that they would be able to release every aspect of their hearts to the Lord.

✓ **They, collectively being rooted and grounded in love, would be able to comprehend, collectively (as a body), and to know the love of Christ:**

> > the width of His love,
> > the length of His love,
> > the depth of His love, and
> > the height of His love.

Paul used two different words for how he wanted the Ephesian saints to take in the love of Christ. First, that they would *comprehend* His love. This means to mentally or intellectually understand it. Second, that they would *know* His love. This means to know through personal experience.

✓ **They would be filled with *"all the fullness of God."***

When we see this, it is hard to comprehend everything that is included in *"all the fullness of God."* Anytime we see the word *all*, we ask, "How much is included in *all?"* The answer, of course, is *everything!* Paul is asking God to totally fill them—throughout every ounce of their being, both individually and corporately—with the richest measure of God's divine presence. These words give the idea of a body wholly filled and flooded with God Himself.

Paul offers reminders to the church:

✓ **God is able to do exceedingly abundantly above all they ask or think, according to (by) the power (Holy Spirit) that is working in their lives.**

✓ **God's glory *"in the church"* is the end result.**

As you read through the points that outline Paul's prayer, did you notice the completeness of the request? Paul followed

God's call on his life each day. And in this detailed prayer, we see he prayed that the Ephesian church would *"be filled with **all** the fullness of God"* as they lived out and followed the call as a body—corporately.

> *Paul did not want the Ephesian believers to live below or miss out on what had been given to them in Christ.*

Paul loved the church at Ephesus and wanted to remind those believers of who they were in Christ and what was available for them to walk worthy of the call God had placed upon their lives when He saved them. The magnitude of this prayer is overwhelming. But Paul prayed as one who had personally experienced God's fullness, and he did not want the Ephesian believers to live below or miss out on what had been given to them *in Christ*.

This prayer is very familiar to most Christians, and the last portion—*"exceedingly abundantly above all that we ask or think"*—is quoted so often. But do we really believe this? When God comes to our lives and sets in motion His claim on our lives, do we respond with the understanding of this prayer? Paul knew from personal experience that God would indeed do everything he had prayed for in the lives of the Ephesian church as they lived out the call. Nothing would be lacking as they served their Lord!

The same thing is true for our lives and churches today. God does not want us to miss His call; He wants us to hear His call, respond obediently, and live, experiencing His power doing exceedingly abundantly above all that we ask or think!

PRAYER & APPLICATION

The inner desire to know God's call and to completely do it is granted to every believer. Describe in your spiritual journal how God is placing in you a desire to know and live out the call.

INVOLVING YOUR CHURCH IN THE CALL

When you are a Christian living in the world, God is actively at work in your life. The moment you begin to sense an inner desire to do the will of God, recognize that this is the activity of God in your life causing you to want to do His will. The activity of God may be experienced while you are studying the Bible, or when you are worshipping in your church, or when you are praying, or in the midst of your daily routine, or even when you are talking with a friend or one of your family members. There are some things that only God can do. Creating awareness of His call is something only God can do in a believer's life.

> *Creating awareness of His call is something only God can do in a believer's life.*

Once you are aware of God's call on your life, share it with your church. Let's look at two examples and the results of such sharing.

FROM HENRY: GOD'S INVITATION TO HELP LONELY PARENTS

Bill and Anne responded in a very different manner than did other people when our community learned that a policeman in our city had been murdered. The two young men who committed the crime were arrested, and the anger of the people in the city mounted. But during our prayer meeting, Bill and Anne began to weep as they shared a deep burden in their hearts for the parents of the young men arrested. They themselves had a son in jail and knew the pain and loneliness such parents feel. As they shared their hearts, the entire church family began to understand and feel their pain, too. We knew God was speaking to us through them.

Bill and Anne asked that we pray for them, because they had invited the parents of these two boys to their home for coffee. They had also told the parents of their concern and God's personal love and concern. We agreed to pray.

The parents of the two boys cried out, "We have been hated and cursed at by others. You are the only persons who have cared about our hurt. Thank you!"

Out of this experience, our church family, along with Bill and Anne, began an extensive jail ministry—to both the inmates in several jails and prisons and their parents and families. Our entire church became involved in ministry to inmates and their families. Why? Because two believers knew they were children of a loving God and knew that God was calling them to respond. God wanted to work through them and their church in the lives of others who were hurting. One of our mission churches was even begun with families of prison inmates.

FROM HENRY: MINISTERING TO THE DISABLED

The prayer meetings had become very special for Cathy. In the meetings, as she prayed, she often sensed the moving of God in her life, giving her clear direction.

One Wednesday evening she shared, "God has given me a great burden for ministering to the mentally and physically disadvantaged and their families. I grew up with a mentally handicapped sister. I know what this does to the parents and the family. No one in the churches of our city is ministering to these people. I sense we should seek God's guidance to see if we should be involved." The more she shared and the more we prayed, the more our hearts came together as one (Matthew 18:19–20).

We became convinced that God was directing not only Cathy but also our entire church to become involved. To us it was a clear call of God, and we felt accountable to God to respond. We did, and Cathy helped us know what to do. Soon we had 15 to 20 mentally challenged young adults attending church with us along with some of their family members.

Through involvement with these special people, our church came to experience more of the meaning of pure love than we had ever experienced before. God called Cathy and her church as she prayed and then as we prayed with her, and God began to accomplish His loving purposes through us.

In these two examples, God spoke to individuals, who then shared God's call on their lives with their church. And just as Paul prayed in Ephesians 3, God received glory in the church as the whole body of believers helped these individuals live out the call.

Living out the call of God will involve those around you in your local church. This truth is clearly seen in many Scriptures; for example, this passage from Matthew 18:

> *"Again I say to you that if two of you agree on earth concerning anything that they ask, it will be done for them by My Father in heaven. For where two or three are gathered together in My name, I am there in the midst of them."*
>
> —MATTHEW 18:19–20

God promises that He will be *"in the midst of"* those who are gathered together in agreement in His name.

Being in agreement is foundational as you live out your life in the body of Christ alongside other Christians.

In Romans, Paul instructs Christians to **live in harmony and humility:**

Live in harmony with one another; do not be haughty (snob-bish, high-minded, exclusive), but readily adjust yourself to [people, things] and give yourselves to humble tasks. Never overestimate yourself or be wise in your own conceits.

—ROMANS 12:16 (AMP)

In 1 Corinthians, Paul urges believers to **be united in perfect harmony:**

But I urge and entreat you, brethren, by the name of our Lord Jesus Christ, that all of you be in perfect harmony and full agreement in what you say, and that there be no dissen-sions or factions or divisions among you, but that you be perfectly united in your common understanding and in your opinions and judgments.

—1 CORINTHIANS 1:10 (AMP)

Finally, this declaration from Peter challenges Christians to **be of the same mind:**

Finally, all [of you] should be of one and the same mind (united in spirit), sympathizing [with one another], loving [each other] as brethren [of one household], compassionate and courte-ous (tenderhearted and humble). Never return evil for evil or insult for insult (scolding, tongue-lashing, berating), but on the contrary blessing [praying for their welfare, happiness, and protection, and truly pitying and loving them]. For know that to this you have been called, that you may yourselves inherit

a blessing [from God—that you may obtain a blessing as heirs,
bringing welfare and happiness and protection].

—1 Peter 3:8–9 (AMP)

The Scriptures are clear with regard to how Christians are to relate to each other as they serve God together. Read the previous four passages of Scripture again and circle the words that describe how the body of Christ should relate to one another. (If you don't want to mark in your book, make a list in your journal.) Here are the relational instructions we noted in Matthew 18:19–20; Romans 12:16; 1 Corinthians 1:10; and 1 Peter 3:8–9:

- ✓ Agree (Matthew 18:19–20).
- ✓ Live in harmony (Romans 12:16).
- ✓ Do not be haughty, snobbish, high-minded, or exclusive (Romans 12:16).
- ✓ Readily adjust to people and things (Romans 12:16).
- ✓ Take on humble tasks (Romans 12:16).
- ✓ Never overestimate yourself (Romans 12:16).
- ✓ Be in perfect harmony and full agreement (1 Corinthians 1:10).
- ✓ Have no dissensions or factions or divisions (1 Corinthians 1:10).
- ✓ Be perfectly united in common understanding, in opinions, and in judgments (1 Corinthians 1:10).

✓ Be of one and the same mind, united in spirit (1 Peter 3:8–9).

✓ Sympathize with one another (1 Peter 3:8–9).

✓ Love each other as brethren of one household (1 Peter 3:8–9).

✓ Be compassionate and courteous, tenderhearted and humble (1 Peter 3:8–9).

✓ Never return evil for evil or insult for insult (1 Peter 3:8–9).

✓ Return blessing for evil (1 Peter 3:8–9):

- Pray for the welfare, happiness, and protection of the evildoer.
- Truly pity and love the evildoer.

BEARING WITNESS TO THE CALL

When you recognize God's call on your life, it is important to bear witness to the call of God and to testify as to how He is causing you to live out this call.

FROM HENRY: GOD AT WORK!

Terry worked for a very significant microchip company. As Terry studied his Bible, prayed, and worshipped regularly, God began to speak to him. During a worship service, Terry came forward indicating that God was calling him to be a more effective witness in his place of work.

"But," he said, "my desk is out of the way at the end of a hall and only one person comes by my office. How can God use me to witness to the many in my office?"

I shared his sense of call with the church, and we pledged to pray with him. I encouraged him to look carefully for the activity of God in answer to our prayer and to be prepared to obey immediately. It was not long before he joyfully shared with the church: "This week my boss came to me and said, 'Terry, I want to move your desk. I hope you don't mind!' My desk now is in the busiest place in the office, right at the drinking fountain, the copier, and the coffee center. Everybody comes by my desk now. Please pray for me that I will be the faithful witness God has called me to be in my workplace!"

> *When we bear witness to the call of God and then live out the call among God's people, it will serve as an encouragement to others to step out in faith to serve God.*

This experience caused the entire church to be more sensitive to God's call in their lives, as well as to the church.

When we bear witness to the call of God and then live out the call among God's people, it will serve as an encouragement to others to step out in faith to serve God. God will not let you miss His call on your life or your church when you are intentionally listening to Him and abiding in His love. God often uses your local church family to help you understand His call as well as live out this call. Let's look at a few examples of this truth from the Scriptures.

The Book of Philemon is Paul's shortest letter recorded in Scripture; he wrote it to Philemon to let him know that Onesimus (Philemon's runaway slave) had become a true follower of Jesus Christ. However, before addressing the issue of Onesimus in this letter, Paul greets his beloved friend and acknowledges Philemon's life of service: *"For we have great joy and consolation in your love, because the hearts of the saints have been refreshed by you, brother"* (v. 7). Philemon is described as one who refreshes the hearts of the saints. How would your fellow church members describe your life as you live out the call of God on your life? Could they say, "That person's life always refreshes and brings joy to my life"?

When Paul heard of the testimony of the Colossian church, he gave *"thanks to the God and Father of our Lord Jesus Christ"* (Colossians 1:3). What do other churches in your community do when they hear your church's name?

Paul continually shared with the early churches about the way in which he was living out the call of God. He was careful to share his life and call with the early church to encourage them, to set an example, and to stir them to follow the call of God in their own lives and churches (Philippians 1:12–18; 1 Thessalonians 2:1–12; 1 Timothy 1:12–17).

Many times people around you have a desire to follow God but are afraid to step out in faith. As you follow God and share how God is working in your life, your testimony serves as a source of encouragement to other individuals who may be hesitant to release their own lives to God. Sharing your calling with your church and living out this call among the fellowship of the church serves as an encouragement to the entire church body.

PRAYER & APPLICATION

Can you think of a person in your church whose life and devotion to Christ serve as a source of encouragement to the rest of the church? How has this person's life impacted your own life? Take a moment today and thank God for this person. You might also consider writing him or her a note of encouragement this week.

In what ways have you allowed your life to serve as an encouragement for others in your church to follow after Christ?

DAILY LIVING THE CALL

How do you live out the call of God in your life? It begins and is sustained in your daily relationship with God, from the beginning of the day to the end of the day!

David's life provides a great example for us. In Psalm 63, we see how David described his relationship with God. Let's take a moment to read it:

1 O God, You are my God; early will I seek You; my soul thirsts for You; my flesh longs for You in a dry and thirsty land where there is no water.

2 So I have looked for You in the sanctuary, to see Your power and Your glory.

3 Because Your lovingkindness is better than life, my lips shall praise You.

4 Thus I will bless You while I live; I will lift up my hands in Your name.

5 My soul shall be satisfied as with marrow and fatness, and my mouth shall praise You with joyful lips.

6 When I remember You on my bed, I meditate on You in the night watches.

7 Because You have been my help, therefore in the shadow of Your wings I will rejoice.

8 My soul follows close behind You; Your right hand upholds me.

9 But those who seek my life, to destroy it, shall go into the lower parts of the earth.

10 They shall fall by the sword; they shall be a portion for jackals.

11 But the king shall rejoice in God; everyone who swears by Him shall glory; but the mouth of those who speak lies shall be stopped.

—PSALM 63

David described, with passion, the way he sought the Lord. He shared how his soul thirsted for God and desired to see His power and glory (vv. 1–2); he longed to experience God's loving-kindness (v. 3) and to have his soul satisfied by God (v. 5). Because God had been his help (v. 7), David rejoiced in the protection he experienced being under God's wing (v. 7).

Can you see why David would seek after God in the process of living out his life as God's servant? God continues to watch over His people daily! And those who have come to walk intimately with God throughout the day and night can certainly identify with David in this psalm.

In your quiet time alone with God at the beginning of the day, God speaks to you and guides you to know and understand what He is planning to do that day through where He has your life.

If you close this time by saying, "O God, please go with me this day and bless me!" God may say something like this to you: "You have it backwards! I have a will and plan for what I want to do through your life today. I want *you* to go with *Me*, so I am alerting you now through My Word and your praying to know My will for you, so you can partner with Me today!"

In your same quiet time, the Lord Jesus will bring to your heart the full assurance that whatever the Father has in mind, He (Jesus) will be present with you and in you to provide all the resources you will need to see the Father's will fulfilled through you. In addition to that, the Holy Spirit will be giving His assurance that He will enable you to implement in your life this specific will of God and any call of God! What an incredible privilege! What an awesome responsibility! What an accountability we have to love Him, believe Him, trust Him, and obey Him! It is then that you will experience the wonderful presence and power of God working His will in you and through you.

Ask not what you can do for God, but what God is doing in you!

Now, because you know that God is working in you and will complete what He has begun, you should live with a clear sense of expectation and anticipation of God doing this in your life daily. Ask not what you can do for God, but what God is doing in you! What He begins, He Himself will bring to completion.

How encouraging it is to read in Isaiah this promise from God:

> *The LORD of hosts has sworn, saying,*
> *"Surely, as I have thought, so it shall come to pass,*
> *And as I have purposed, so it shall stand. . . .*
> *For the LORD of hosts has purposed,*
> *And who will annul it?*
> *His hand is stretched out,*
> *And who will turn it back?"*
> —ISAIAH 14:24, 27

And then read the words of Jeremiah, as he describes what the Lord said about His thoughts:

*For I know the **thoughts** that I think toward you, says the*
*LORD, **thoughts** of peace and not of evil, to give you a future*
and a hope. Then you will call upon Me and go and pray
to Me, and I will listen to you. And you will seek Me and
find Me, when you search for Me with all your heart. I will
be found by you, says the LORD, and I will bring you back
from your captivity; I will gather you from all the nations and
from all the places where I have driven you, says the LORD,
and I will bring you to the place from which I cause you to be
carried away captive.

—JEREMIAH 29:11–14

Now, let's look at how David describes the **thoughts** our
heavenly Father has towards His children.

*How precious also are Your **thoughts** to me, O God!*
How great is the sum of them!
If I should count them, they would be more in number than
the sand;
When I awake, I am still with You.

—PSALM 139:17–18

When you read these verses, does it give you confidence that the
Lord, who called you, will complete everything He has purposed
to do in and through your life?

Let's summarize:

- God's thoughts toward you outnumber the sand on the seashore.
- His thoughts are *"thoughts of peace and not of evil, to give you a future and a hope."*
- When God thinks a thought toward you, *"it shall come to pass."*
- When the Lord has *"purposed"* something, no one *"will annul it"*!

Do you have any current decisions to make in your walk with God, but you have been hesitant to step out in faith because you cannot foresee the outcome? If so, write the decisions in your spiritual journal and then ask God to apply the Isaiah passage discussed (14:24, 27) to your situation.

> *Once God has spoken to your heart, it is as good as done, for God has never spoken to reveal His will and not Himself guaranteed the completion of what He has said.*

Once God has spoken to your heart, it is as good as done, for God has never spoken to reveal His will and not Himself guaranteed the completion of what He has said. This will be as true for you as for anyone in the Bible or history. You can be absolutely confident that once God has begun a work in you or revealed where He wants you to join Him in His work, He will be faithful to carry the work to its completion.

Take a moment to meditate on the following Scriptures, and notice how they describe God and how He fulfills His Word and completes His work. Once you have studied these Scriptures, ask God to apply them to current events and decisions you are facing.

6 *Seek, inquire for, and require the Lord while He may be found [claiming Him by necessity and by right]; call upon Him while He is near.*

7 *Let the wicked forsake his way and the unrighteous man his thoughts; and let him return to the Lord, and He will have love, pity, and mercy for him, and to our God, for He will multiply to him His abundant pardon.*

8 *For My thoughts are not your thoughts, neither are your ways My ways, says the Lord.*

9 *For as the heavens are higher than the earth, so are My ways higher than your ways and My thoughts than your thoughts.*

10 *For as the rain and snow come down from the heavens, and return not there again, but water the earth and make it bring forth and sprout, that it may give seed to the sower and bread to the eater,*

11 *So shall My word be that goes forth out of My mouth: it shall not return to Me void [without producing any effect, useless], but it shall accomplish that which I please and purpose, and it shall prosper in the thing for which I sent it.*

12 *For you shall go out [from the spiritual exile caused by sin and evil into the homeland] with joy and be led forth [by your Leader, the Lord Himself, and His word] with peace; the mountains and the hills shall break forth before you into singing, and all the trees of the field shall clap their hands.*

13 *Instead of the thorn shall come up the cypress tree, and instead of the brier shall come up the myrtle tree; and it shall be to the Lord for a name of renown, for an everlasting sign [of jubilant exaltation] and memorial [to His praise], which shall not be cut off.*

—ISAIAH 55:6–13 (AMP)

"God is not a man, that He should lie,
Nor a son of man, that He should repent.
Has He said, and will He not do?
Or has He spoken, and will He not make it good?"

--NUMBERS 23:19

How confident can you be that the Lord will fulfill all He has purposed for your life based on these Scriptures?

THE JOY OF LIVING OUT THE CALL OF GOD

So often we look at the call of God on our lives and tend to focus on the work ahead or the sacrifices involved. While there is much labor involved and many sacrifices along the way, these things do not compare to the joy that comes from following the call of God.

Jesus urged the disciples to remain or abide in His love by keeping His commandments, and by doing this, they would remain in the love of the Father (John 15:9–10; 14:23). However, He went on to say that the reason He was telling them to do this was so that His joy would remain in them and that their joy would be full (John 15:11).

> *"As the Father loved Me, I also have loved you; abide in My love. If you keep My commandments, you will abide in My love, just as I have kept My Father's commandments and abide in His love. These things I have spoken to you, that **My joy may remain in you, and that your joy may be full**."*
> —JOHN 15:9–11 (BOLD ADDED)

When we follow God's leading in our lives and submit ourselves to His will, the result is that we experience the joy of Christ in our lives. As Jesus prayed for His disciples as recorded in John 17, He said He spoke certain things in the world so that they would have His joy fulfilled in their lives.

> *"But now I come to You [the Father], and these things I speak in the world, that they may have My joy fulfilled in themselves."*
> —JOHN 17:13

In addition, great joy comes from living out the call in the midst of God's people. If you think back over the times you have been overwhelmed with joy or excited because of something good, most often you can hardly wait to tell others the good news. It is wonderful to be able to share good things with others. An excitement is generated by serving God together as His "called out" people.

FROM HENRY: THE JOY OF SERVING TOGETHER

In the church, we experience together the excitement of being on mission. Ministry to the down-and-out, to the school system, to the jails, to the mentally and physically handicapped, to the university, to the Indian reservations, to the surrounding towns and villages, and even to the ends of the earth was experienced by the members of our church. Everyone became involved, individually as well as corporately as a body, with God in His activity. Many felt called to be pastors or church staff; others felt called to minister in other countries of the world; still others gained a clear sense of a call to serve, witness, and minister in the marketplace and the homes where God had placed them. Together we helped each other to be accountable—first to God, who had called us, and then to each other—as we sought to be the body of Christ

> *Everyone became involved, individually as well as corporately as a body, with God in His activity.*

in our world through which the Father could and would carry out His purposes.

Great joy comes when you are on mission with God and with His people! And along with this joy comes a great accountability to God. Certainly the parable of the talents found in Matthew 25:14–30 is a warning. We will give an account for all God has called us to do and equipped us to accomplish. Paul challenged the Corinthians that each one's work or service to God would be made clear before God.

> *A call to salvation is a call to be on mission with our Lord. This call is not just for a select few, but to all who are called to a relationship with Christ.*

Each one's work will become clear; for the Day will declare it, because it will be revealed by fire; and the fire will test each one's work, of what sort it is. If anyone's work which he has built on it endures, he will receive a reward. If anyone's work is burned, he will suffer loss; but he himself will be saved, yet so as through fire.

—1 Corinthians 3:13–15

A call to salvation is a call to be on mission with our Lord. This call is not just for a select few, but to all who are called to a relationship with Christ. At the moment of salvation, every Christian enters into a relationship with Jesus in which

He becomes our Lord and we become His servant. We never have to look or wait for some kind of special or separate call of God to serve Him. As Christians, we are given one life to live. How tragic it would be for us to waste the opportunity to be a co-worker with Jesus Christ in our generation! Answering the call of God brings joy and indescribable satisfaction to a Christian's heart. As Christians, we are also privileged to serve God together in the local church setting and, thereby, to share His joy and fulfillment with others.

PRAYER & APPLICATION

In 2 Corinthians 5:10, Paul states, *"For we must all appear before the judgment seat of Christ, that each one may receive the things done in the body, according to what he has done, whether good or bad."*

Have you been living your life with the understanding that one day you will give an account for how you used your life, either in service to God or looking out for self? How has this understanding shaped the way you order your goals and priorities?

Conclusion

We hope you have come to know and experience God as you read each page in this book. We purposefully filled the pages with the Word of God, knowing that His Word will never return void. As we have explained, all Christians are called to be on mission with God in their world and to faithfully live out the call in their generation.

The call of God is a call to a total relationship with Him for the purposes He had for us from before the foundation of the world. God calls us by causing us to want to do His will, and then He enables us to do it. He first calls each of us to be His child by faith in Jesus, His Son. In that relationship, God provides all we need to live fully with Him. That relationship will always involve us joining Him in His redemptive activity in our world. As God works through us, we come to know Him and grow toward Christlikeness. This Christlike character that God develops in us as we grow in the knowledge of Him is what prepares us for eternity with Him.

What a plan and what a purpose God has for each of us! May we respond to Him as He works in us and through us mightily in our generation.

Called and accountable—God's greatest of privileges given freely to every believer!

Index of Scripture References

Books for Missional Living

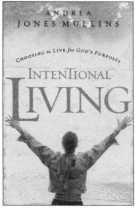

Intentional Living
*Choosing to Live
for God's Purposes*
Andrea Mullins
1-56309-927-6

Fueled by Faith
*Living Vibrantly
in the Power of Prayer*
Jennifer Kennedy Dean
1-56309-993-4

Splash the Living Water
*Sharing Jesus
in Everyday Moments*
Esther Burroughs
1-59669-002-X

Available in bookstores everywhere